God's Grace for the Church

Exposition of Ephesians

Martin Murphy

God's Grace for the Church
Exposition of Ephesians

Copyright © 2018 by Martin Murphy

All rights reserved. No part of this book may be reproduced or transmitted in any form or by any means without written permission of the author.

Unless otherwise noted Scripture is taken from the New King James Version. Copyright © 1979, 1980, 1982 by Thomas Nelson, Inc. Used by permission. All rights reserved.

Library of Congress Control Number: 2018910104

ISBN 9781732437906

TO: The spiritual progeny of the Ephesian Church

Preface

The seed for this book was planted in the Spring of 1991 during my New Testament studies at Reformed Theological Seminary. It was practically an academic exercise. Later I preached through it, then taught from it and eventually took all my notes and began writing this exposition. The book of Ephesians was Paul's letter to the Christian church at Ephesus. The church at Ephesus has a prominent place in the New Testament since it is mentioned in the Book of Acts chapters 19 and 20 and in Revelation chapter 2.

Ephesus was a city in Asia Minor of significance and importance for the spread of the gospel. Ephesus was a large city of about 300,000 at the time of Paul's ministry. Ephesus was a port city bringing people through Ephesus from all parts of the world. It was the home of a theater that would seat an estimated 25,000 people. Ephesus was the home of the temple Diana, which was known as one of the wonders of the ancient world. The city derived wealth and prestige from temple worship. Think of Ephesus in terms of a mega-city, which would be comparable to any large city in the United States.

The effect that Christianity had on the ungodly culture at Ephesus caused some of the Ephesians to instigate a riot to overthrow the peaceful cultural revolution brought on by the gospel. It should be observed that Luke does not use the word church to describe the Christian converts. He describes the Christian converts at Ephesus in terms of "the Way" (Acts 19:23). Christianity was a new way of life. It was the way of the true and living God. The Lord Jesus Christ was at the center of their religious lives. The change was revolutionary bringing a new set of morals and a new way of life called the church.

It was "the Way" (the church) that disturbed the men who made and sold the silver shrines of Diana. The manufacturer of those silver shrines was big business in the city of Ephesus. The ungodly culture at Ephesus depended on the idolatry and worship of the goddess Diana. Christians today may not have the monstrous temple in Ephesus and accompanying financial and economic benefits from it, but they have plenty of other monumental idols that create billions of dollars in the current economy.

The announcement of the gospel and the power of the Holy Spirit, along with the means of grace in preaching the Word of God transformed some of the people of Ephesus. The transformation was significant enough so that it penetrated the entire culture. The people quit buying the silver shrines. The business people were outraged because their pocket books and bank accounts dwindled.

Demetrius, a silversmith in Ephesus, saw the threat of the Christian cultural reform. He gathered the other silversmiths together and collectively they incited some of the citizens of Ephesus to wrath. Demetrius appealed not only to the economic effect, but also to religious motives. "So not only is this trade of ours in danger of falling into disrepute, but also the temple of the great goddess Diana may be despised and her magnificence destroyed, whom all Asia and the world worship" (Acts 19:27). Demetrius wanted to gain the support of the citizens, so that the civil authorities would then have a reason to crush the Christian revolution. The Ephesian Christians demonstrated their faith and commitment to the Word of God. Unfortunately, many professing Christians believe, but they privatize their faith. They keep it at home and leave the public square to the ungodly vultures of cultural tyranny. The cultural relevance of the Christian religion depends on faith and ideals, but it also depends on the practice of Christian principles in the public sector.

When the way of life for the Christian conflicts with another way of life, the battle over cultural authority begins. Cultural authority is the contest between unbelievers and believers. The disrespect for the Christian religion has devolved from one generation to another generation for so long that the decline has robbed Christians of their freedom.

The truth of God's Word will cast its light over the culture. Truth will inspire discipline and constraint upon the culture. The absence of truth from the Word of God will cause cultural collapse and the culture will decline to the point of chaos and confusion.

It is time for professing Christians in this country to invade the culture. If the millions who profess Christianity are merely professing Christians, you may think that the mission is impossible. It is not. Christians are called to be faithful. Noah was faithful with only a few. Abraham was faithful with only one heir. Elijah stood against 100's, Jeremiah against the entire nation. Evidence from Scripture and through 2000 years of church history reveals the myriads of Christians who stood against the odds of the secular dominant culture. A promise accompanied the mission Christ gave the church. The Lord's promise was, "I am with you always, even to the end of the age" (Matthew 28:20).

The religious lies of any culture will not survive against the truth of the Word of God. The truth of the Word of God will expose the emptiness of idolatry and the man-made gods of culture. The truth of the Word of God clearly and calmly proclaimed will transform culture.

The proponents of the modern religious culture will rise up against the gospel, if the gospel interferes with their cultural milieu. They will do it in the name of religious zeal and patriotic pride in an effort to exterminate the gospel of Jesus Christ and consequently the full counsel of God.

God may send someone like the town clerk at Ephesus to give Christians temporary relief (Acts 19:35-41). Many theologians have turned the town clerk at Ephesus into a hero for Christianity. However, the town clerk showed no love for Christianity. All he did was to save the Ephesians from self-destruction. He simply acted according to his nature. He wanted to save himself and his city. He knew very well that an unchecked riot may cause the city of Ephesus to lose its free status in the Roman Empire. The town clerk was merely jealous to save his wicked and perverted culture.

The cultural revolution in Ephesus was the result of Paul and his companion's faithfulness to the mission of the church. They made disciples and taught them the full counsel of God. A peaceful revolution reformed the culture. The change in the Ephesians way of life was the result of their change of heart and mind. If you are reformed by the Word of God and the power of the Holy Spirit, you may cause a cultural revolution.

This book brings the grace of God into focus for everyday life in the church. The primary purpose of the church is to worship and glorify God. It is a brief exposition of Paul's letter to the Ephesians. Paul wrote to the particular church at Ephesus, but it applies to the visible church in every age. The church is the proper place for people to experience the manifestation of God's grace.

The glory of God in the church refers to the manifestation of God in the fullest sense of the word. God's glory reflects the radiant, powerful, just, and holy character shining through to the deepest crevice of the souls of his children.

Martin Murphy
July 27, 2018

Table of Contents

1. The Grace of God in His Great Plan 1
2. The Grace of God in His Redemptive Will 9
3. The Grace of God in Christ 15
4. The Grace of God for Dead Men 21
5. The Grace of God's Love 27
6. The Grace of God's Saving Faith 31
7. The Grace of God in the Blood of Christ 35
8. The Grace of God's Peace 41
9. The Grace of God's Revelation of Christ 47
10. The Grace of God in the Mystery of Christ 53
11. The Grace of God for the Soul of Man 59
12. The Grace of God for Your Call 65
13. The Grace of God for Ministry 71
14. The Grace of God's Truth 77
15. The Grace of God's Commandments 83
16. The Grace of God's Forgiveness 89
17. The Grace of God in His Wrath 95
18. The Grace of God in the Children of Light 101
19. The Grace of God in Wise Living 107
20. The Grace of God in a Godly Marriage 113
21. The Grace of God in Order and Authority 119

22. The Grace of God in His Glorious Power 125
23. The Glory of God's Benediction 131

1. The Grace of God in His Great Plan

Ephesians 1:1-6

Paul's letter to the Ephesian Church is ripe with words of great theological significance. Although every word in the Bible is inspired by the Holy Spirit of God, some words touch the marrow of the human soul. Paul used three words in his letter to the Ephesians that humble and strengthen Christians at the same time. Brief definitions of those three words are necessary to understand the profound character of God and His relationship to His people.

Paul used the word grace twelve times in his letter to the Ephesians. The mention of the word grace throws many professing Christians into a state of confusion. In postmodern times sound bites have replaced theology and biblical doctrine. The sound bite that replaced the theology of God's grace is found in the acronym that comes from the word grace itself:

God's
Riches
At
Christ's
Expense

This sounds like a juvenile terse expression for consumerism rather than the magnificent manifestation of God's love for His church.

Since the Bible was originally written in the Greek language, any word study must begin there. The word grace in the New Testament derives from the Greek noun *charis*, which is also translated into English as blessing, favor, or thankfulness. When *charis* is used as a verb it means to show favor. However, when used in terms of God's eternal decree there is no quid pro quo. God does not expect a favor in return.

The most significant controversy in the Church of Scotland found its roots in the biblical concept we call grace. Marrow controversy began in 1645 with publication of *The Marrow of Modern Divinity*. The Marrow controversy had two sides. Either side was in dispute with the other over their understanding of the gracious gift of salvation to sinners. There are two questions, but only one answer. Is grace a gift from God or is man able to do something to obtain God's grace? One side said Christ is generally offered to all men. All a person has to do is accept His (Christ's) righteousness and that person will be saved. The Marrow men said, "There is a crucified Savior, with all saving benefits, for them to come to feed upon and partake of freely." The other side said: "Christ died for the elect and the gospel is offered in a special way by Christ to the elect." The misunderstanding of this controversy is a misunderstanding of the grace of God and the sinfulness of man. If man is dead in sin, as the Bible so clearly teaches, then man cannot do anything until he receives God's grace for new life in Christ.

The doctrine of God's grace was a major point of doctrinal division for the Roman Catholic Church and the Protestant Church. Since God's grace is an expression of salvation, there is a question that remains unsettled. Is God's grace imputed to the sinner or infused into the sinner?

Rome has taught the infusion of grace for most of its existence. The *Council of Trent* ratified the teaching of infused grace in 1564. Chapter VII on Justification:

> [T]he charity of God is poured forth by the Holy Ghost in the hearts of those who are justified...whence man through Jesus Christ, in whom he is ingrafted, receives in that justification, together with the remission of sins,

all these infused at the same time. (*Council of Trent*, Sixth Session, Chapter VII).

Trent went so far as to declare, "If anyone says that the sinner is justified by faith alone, meaning that nothing else is required to co-operate in order to obtain the grace of justification. . .let him be anathema" (Canon 9, *The Council of Trent*).

Yet the teaching of Scripture is plain and clear: "You are saved by grace through faith in Christ." Evangelicals teach that grace is *imputed*. The Roman Catholic Church affirms that grace is *infused*. However, the controversy still rages. God's grace for the church is a display of His glory in the church.

Paul used the word glory nine times in his letter to the Ephesians. It is evident that a primary theme is the glory of God in the church.

Words may shift slightly in meaning from one context to another. Words do not necessarily maintain continuity of meaning from one generation and culture to the next. Sometimes the shift in the meaning of a word occurs because the author intended it for literal or figurative use, but which one.

The word glory is one of those words that not only shifted in its historical context; it shifted in meaning when it was used in the Bible. When Paul wrote the Ephesians, the Greek word *doxa* translated glory commonly referred to (good) opinion or to think. However, in the New Testament glory expresses majesty and esteemed royalty. The New Testament uses the word glory relative to the honor or excellent character of God.

The biblical concept of glory derives from the Old Testament Hebrew word *kabod*. The basic meaning is *to be heavy* or *weighty*. It was seldom used in a literal sense and almost always used in a figurative sense. So it could be said that a weighty person, figuratively speaking, is one of influence, someone who is honorable and worthy of respect.

So in Ephesians when Paul talks about the glory of God, he is talking about the manifestation of God in the fullest sense of the word. God's glory refers to the radiant, powerful, just, and holy character shining through to the deepest crevice of His church.

The church is the recipient of God's saving grace. The glory of God in the church is the Lord Jesus Christ. A brief definition of the word "church" is necessary to understand Paul's letter to the church located at Ephesus.

This term is often misunderstood, misused, and misrepresented by Christians. It is derived from the Greek word *ecclesia* referring to the "the ones called out." In the early Greek city/democracy, it referred to the assembly of the citizens of a city. The Bible does not give a brief definition of the church. The building where God's people meet to fulfill the collective responsibilities is not the church. Furthermore, it is not possible to "go to church" or "meet for church" or any false notion that the church is a place, institution, or organization. Jesus Christ is the head of the church (Colossians 1:18). The church "which is His body, [is] the fullness of Him who fills all in all" (Ephesians 1:23). Therefore, the church consists of those who belong to the family of God, through the work of Christ, by the power of the Holy Spirit. The purpose of the church is worship (Psalm 95:6). The mission of the church is to make disciples and teach the full counsel of God (Matthew 28:19-20). The ministry of the church is to equip Christians to serve in the body of Christ (Ephesians 4:11-16).

The grace and glory of God are evident in Paul's letter to the Ephesians. My purpose is to examine various doctrinal concepts and principles in the book of Ephesians that apply to the contemporary church.

Ephesians

Paul begins his letter to the Ephesians by bringing attention to the grace of God in predestination. Predestination is not a popular doctrine in the age of the alleged sovereign all powerful man. However, Paul not only used the word predestination in his letter to the Ephesians, he used it three other places in the New Testament (Romans 8:29, 30; 1 Corinthians 2:7). Unfortunately, the doctrine of predestination is not widely received in the modern church. Predestination may appear mysterious to sinful men, however God's Word uses it prominently.

"... Just as He chose us in Him before the foundation of the world, that we should be holy and without blame before Him in love..." (Ephesians 1:4). It will make more sense to explain the pronouns and their connections in this brief text. He (God) chose (elected) us (Paul and the saints at Ephesus plus every Christian for all time) in Him (Christ). Now add verse 5 to the context and it puts more light on the context.

> ... just as He chose us in Him before the foundation of the world, that we should be holy and without blame before Him in love having predestined us to adoption as sons by Jesus Christ to Himself, according to the good pleasure of His will. (Ephesians 1:4-5)

God's predestination is certainly God's great plan for His church. Predestination is nothing more than God's electing love. "In love he predestined us." Predestination is another way of saying that the believer's salvation, from first to last, is a work of God. Although the language of Scripture is plain, many professing Christians take exception to the doctrine of predestination.

Perhaps the protest against the predestination doctrine by professing Christians is really a protest against God's authority and sovereignty. The sinful nature of man rejects God's authority. Everyone is infected with sinful self-centeredness.

That alone is enough to leave predestination and election to God's secret counsel. Yes, predestination is off limits for human inquiry. God's people were predestined before the foundation of the world. There are certain things that God reserves for Himself and predestination is one of them. Before God created the world, He knew who His people were because He predested them for His own glory. However, the doctrine of predestination does not exclude anyone from God's saving grace. "Believe on the Lord Jesus Christ, and you will be saved..." (Acts16:31). This mystery is best left in the hands God's sovereign love, compassion, and grace.

The question is often asked: Why did God choose a people for Himself? Was he lonely? No, God is independent. God chose His people so they would be holy and without blame before Him. It did not contribute to or take away from His nature and character.

Some teachers believe, "holy and without blame" in this text refers to sanctification. Some would go so far as to use it as a proof text for perfectionism. According to Roman, Wesleyan and Arminian doctrine, the second work of grace produces holiness and then one is without blame or to put it another way moral perfection has been achieved.

The rest of the Bible, sound reason, and common sense tells me that "to be holy and without blame" refers to our justification. When God justifies His people they are declared righteous in His sight because of Christ. It all boils down to this: God predestined His people (the church) because He loved them.

After all is said and done, I'm still perplexed that people look so negatively on predestination. Those who object to the doctrine of predestination do so on the basis that it is unbecoming of God to condemn so many innocent people to eternal perdition. The first and most prominent theological error is to believe there are "innocent people."

Ephesians

One time I'd like to hear someone say "bless God for his divine purpose so that a great number of people are eternally saved. The church should be grateful for God's divine initiative. Sinners left to themselves would never choose God.

But thank goodness, it was "the good pleasure of God's will" that He predestined His church to be holy and without blame.

The 17th Article of the 39 Articles of the Anglican Church describes predestination as "full of sweet, pleasant, and unspeakable comfort." The doctrine of predestination is not prohibitive and offensive resulting in a sad melancholy state of being. Quite on the contrary. Predestination is full of joy, peace, and forgiveness. In God's predestinating love, He has graciously poured out His blessing to the church in Christ. God's blessing is filled with intelligent, emotional, and willing displays of his wisdom and power. God's blessing is spiritual resulting in eternal life.

God's church will find grace in His great plan.

2. The Grace of God in His Redemptive Will

Ephesians 1:7-14

Redemption is one of those biblical/theological words used by Christian preachers and teachers, but often not understood by laymen. The verb form is redeem, which refers to the payment for a pledged object. For instance, if someone owed the mortgage company for a piece of real estate and failed to make payments, the mortgage company would foreclose and take possession of the property. Then the original owner may be able to redeem the property by paying the mortgage company. If the original owner did not have the financial resources, a third party may recover the property for the owner by means of a ransom payment.

Paul wrote the church, "In Him (Christ) we (the church) have redemption through His (Christ) blood, the forgiveness of sins according to the riches of His (God the Father) grace..." (Ephesians 1:7).

The substance of Paul's brief statement may be understood in light of the doctrine of salvation. The need for salvation comes from the sinful nature of the human race. The inspired apostle Paul makes it very clear that "through one man's offense [Adam's sin] judgment came to all men, resulting in condemnation" (Romans 5:18). The imputation (legal representation) of Adam's sin is often misunderstood. Please notice that "the guilt" of Adam's sin was imputed, not the sin itself. The unsaved sinner is helpless and self-salvation is not possible. The sinful estate of mankind creates a vast chasm between God and man, so vast that mankind is hopelessly doomed without the grace of God. The distance is so great that man can never work his way to God. The sinner may be redeemed, but the ransom required was a perfect sacrifice. Jesus Christ paid the perfect price owed by the sinner. Christ paid with His unblemished perfect life and death on the cross. The *Westminster Confession of Faith* describes the redemptive work of Christ.

> To all those for whom Christ has purchased redemption, He does certainly and effectually apply and communicate the same; making intercession for them, and revealing unto them, in and by the word, the mysteries of salvation; effectually persuading them by His Spirit to believe and obey, and governing their hearts by His word and Spirit; overcoming all their enemies by His almighty power and wisdom, in such manner, and ways, as are most consonant to His wonderful and unsearchable dispensation. (*Westminster Confession of Faith*, chapter 8, section 8).

It is a sin and disgrace for the Christian church to hide the doctrines and beliefs taught in the Bible behind cunningly devised phrases and meaningless words and trusting empty headed theologians with matters of eternal importance.

A cursory reading of Ephesians is sufficient to dispel the idea that man can redeem himself. It is abundantly clear that the Apostle Paul wants the church to see the glory of God in His redemptive will. The glory of God reflects the manifestation of God in the fullest sense of the word. God's glory describes His supreme authority, power, and influence.

Since the fall of our first parents, we, the children of Adam and Eve, want to exert our authority, power, and influence and bring glory to ourselves. However, the very thought of redemption and ultimately the forgiveness of sins, removes the notion that human beings possess the power of eternal salvation.

The doctrine of predestination is central to a biblical understanding of redemption and forgiveness. Paul wrote to the Christians at Ephesus however, Paul's letter applies to the church throughout history. He wrote, "we [the church] have redemption." We have redemption because "we [the church] have obtained an inheritance, being predestined according to the purpose of Him who works all things according to the counsel of His will..." (Ephesians 1:11).

Predestination is a biblical doctrine that teaches the ultimate destiny of all created things was fixed by God before the creation of the world. This doctrine shows the absolute authority of God over all of creation; The term is *God's sovereignty*. The fall of man destined all of humanity to everlasting punishment, but it is the loving sovereign plan of God to save all those who turn to Him in faith and repentance. The grace of God in His redemptive will should be the pinnacle of joy for every redeemed soul. Unfortunately, there are many professing Christians claiming it is their will that redeems the dead soul.

I not only want God to predestine me, I want God to redeem me and God to forgive my sins. God, unlike human beings, is not confused, capricious or careless. Trust God only with the eternal state of the soul.

The doctrine of redemption and forgiveness is inseparable. Jesus Christ gave His life to redeem His church for the glory of God. Paul explains in graphic terms, "We have redemption through the blood of Christ." He paid the penalty for the sins of those whom God called to Himself. The result is the forgiveness of sins.

The source of redemption and forgiveness is God's mysterious, but abundant grace. The word grace has a variety of synonyms associated with it. The word grace essentially refers to the "undeserved favor of God given to sinful man."

This is not only a theological doctrine; it is the experience of God's church. "His (God's) grace which He (God) made to abound toward us in all wisdom and prudence..." (Ephesians 1:7b-8).

Wisdom and prudence is relative to a correct biblical understanding of God's grace. The English word wisdom is derived from the Greek word *Sophia*. It embraces every category of human life. The English word prudence is derived from the Greek word *phronesis* that refers to the proper use of the mind to establish a way of thinking. Grace is rational and experiential. God's grace affects the mind, emotions, and in some sense the will. Abundant grace refers to God's grace touching the whole soul.

The promise of eternal salvation is worthless unless the professing Christian has an assurance of eternal salvation. Unless professing Christians come to understand the root or foundation of redemption, forgiveness and grace, they will not embrace an infallible assurance of eternal salvation. The doctrine of assurance is not merely grounded in feckless hope, but from rational evidence in the Word of God and the work of the Holy Spirit.

One of the grounds of assurance is the infallible truth and another is the promise of salvation. Another ground of infallible assurance is the inward evidence of those graces unto which these promises are made. The inward evidence includes every aspect of sanctification and the spiritual maturity of the believer. The third ground of assurance mentioned is the testimony of the Spirit of adoption witnessing with our spirit that we are children of God. God speaks to the church in terms of, "he who believes in the Son of God has the witness in himself" (1 John 5:10). The final ground of assurance is the work of the Holy Spirit sealed unto the day of redemption. Feelings and emotions are not the grounds of assurance.

Ephesians

Paul's letter to the church reveals the extent of God's grace. "In Him also we have obtained an inheritance, being predestined according to the purpose of Him who works all things according to the counsel of His will" (Ephesians 1:11). What determines our destiny? Not fate, not our human resourcefulness, not our ability, and not anything associated with the human will. It is the will of God, the secret will of God that determines our destiny. There are some things about God's will that we can know. We know that it is His will to save some people for His own glory, not that they or anyone deserve salvation. There are some things about God's will that we cannot know. We cannot know the names of the people who will be saved except they are called the elect and they are objects of God's grace.

There are some people who suggest that God's redemption is universal. God's redemption is universal in that it includes absolutely everything that has ever, is now and ever will be taking place on earth, in heaven, in hell, for believers and unbelievers, to angels and devils, physical and spiritual beings or anything else in reality.

God's unsearchable redemptive will was predetermined before the foundation of the world and it is the doctrine of providence that brings his redemptive will into focus in our everyday lives. The things we see working together is the revelation of God's divine energy being poured out in this present world.

The phrase "the counsel of his will" deserves more attention. The English word counsel derives from the Greek word *boule*. In this text it refers to God's purpose in the destiny of all things including the final destiny of the human race. The English word will derives from the Greek word *thelo*. It refers to God making plans without reference to any outside source.

God's will from all eternity is all embracing. If His will is fully carried out in history and if His children are included in

His plan, then Christians have no reason to boast. So it follows that God's chosen people are justified and adopted as sons of the living God for no other purpose than to glorify God. Christians have no reason to boast according to their human pride and arrogance, but they have every reason to glorify God in His redemptive will.

3. The Grace of God in Christ

Ephesians 1:15-23

The centerpiece of God's great work among men is Jesus Christ. This text of Scripture intensifies and magnifies the grace of God in Christ. His great work reveals the grace of God in the church on earth. Paul's emphasis in Ephesians is on the relationship of God the Father to God the Son. Paul highlights "your faith in the Lord Jesus" (Ephesians 1:15). Paul prays that the grace of God will give the church, "the knowledge of Him" (Ephesians 1:17). The church should rejoice because, "He [God] raised Him [Jesus Christ] from the dead and seated Him at His right hand in the heavenly places…" (Ephesians 1:20).

Paul's letter to the Colossian Church describes the grace of God in Christ in majestic terms.

> He has delivered us from the power of darkness and conveyed us into the kingdom of the Son of His love, in whom we have redemption through His blood, the forgiveness of sins. He is the image of the invisible God, the firstborn over all creation. For by Him all things were created that are in heaven and that are on earth, visible and invisible, whether thrones or dominions or principalities or powers. All things were created through Him and for Him. And He is before all things, and in Him all things consist. And He is the head of the body, the church, who is the beginning, the firstborn from the dead, that in all things He may have the preeminence. (Colossians 1:13-18)

The ungodly secular culture seeks to remove the Christ of the Bible from the public square and everything that Christians should hold dear. They try to rob Christ of His deity and His divine nature. They may see Him as a good man, but not the second person of the Trinity. They try to rob Him of His essence and divine character. They do not recognize His self-existence and the source of all being. They do not acknowledge His authority and power.

The evangelical church has compromised and failed to defend the Lord and giver of life in the face of the ungodly secular culture. Christ represents His people; He saved them from the power of darkness and set them free in Christ. What a marvelous supernatural act of grace that released the church from the authority of Satan. However, the soul of man has limited ability to understand the nature, character, authority, and power of Christ because of the sinful human nature. John Calvin correctly said, "The finite cannot (fully) comprehend the infinite."

The greatest gift God gave the human race was a functional rational intelligent mind. The greatest gift God gave the church is Jesus Christ. The human race, with the exception of mental defects, has rational powers; however, they may not properly employ them. Only the church, true Christians, enjoy the saving grace of Jesus Christ. The grace of God in Jesus Christ belongs only to the children of God.

> Jesus said to them [the religious leaders of Israel], "If God were your Father, you would love Me, for I proceeded forth and came from God; nor have I come of Myself, but He sent Me. Why do you not understand My speech? Because you are not able to listen to My word. You are of your father the devil, and the desires of your father you want to do. He was a murderer from the beginning, and does not stand in the truth, because there is no truth in him. When he speaks a lie, he

speaks from his own resources, for he is a liar and the father of it. But because I tell the truth, you do not believe Me. Which of you convicts Me of sin? And if I tell the truth, why do you not believe Me? He who is of God hears God's words; therefore you do not hear, because you are not of God." (John 8:42-47)

Throughout the history of the church men and women have given their life and attention to the study of Jesus Christ; however, many of them never come to understand the grace of God in Jesus Christ. Ask the average person on the street, "who has been the most influential religious person in history?" You may receive a variety of answers like evangelist Billy Graham; Martin Luther King Jr.; Norman Vincent Peale; Joel Osteen or some other celebrity religious leader. How many would say, "Jesus Christ?"

I wonder if the Apostle Paul could write your local church today and say I've heard of your faith in the Lord Jesus. Would he pray with the passion with which he prayed for the church at Ephesus? You must answer those questions yourself. However, it is certain Paul prayed that the church may have a spirit of wisdom and revelation. A spirit of wisdom denotes good and honorable knowledge derived from the natural world. Paul's use of the word revelation is "in the knowledge of Him" (Ephesians 1:17). The church will understand and experience the grace of God in Christ when the church seeks the full knowledge of Jesus Christ.

Has your heart been enlightened? Paul prayed for the enlightenment of the hearts for the Christians in Ephesus. Some New Testament scholars say that the enlightenment is in opposition to wisdom and revelation. However, it is the grace of God in Christ that enlightens or illumines your mind.

Jesus alludes to the enlightened mind in Luke 11:29ff. Some of the people following Jesus questioned the authority of Jesus immediately after Jesus drove out a demon from a man who was mute - a man unable to carry on intelligent human discourse. Then some of those present asked for a sign from heaven. How absurd! They had just seen a sign, but did they see a sign? Jesus explains:

> The lamp of the body is the eye. Therefore, when your eye is good, your whole body also is full of light. But when your eye is bad, your body also is full of darkness. Therefore take heed that the light, which is in you, is not darkness. If then your whole body is full of light, having no part dark, the whole body will be full of light, as when the bright shining of a lamp gives you light." (Luke 11:34-36)

God reveals His creative power in the natural physical world. All rational creatures see His creative power. His redeemed church will see His glory, majesty, dignity, nature and character from the Word of God. Then God illumines or causes the renewed mind to comprehend those things He reveals. If professing Christians have faith, real faith, then their whole existence is for the glory of God in Christ. Paul said God raised Christ from the dead and seated Him at His right hand in the heavenly places.

Pietism, moralism, and liberalism influenced most of the Bible belt churches to the extent that those churches read the Bible searching for the glory of man in Christ. God is far above anything we might attempt to describe. Paul describes Christ as "far above" literally "beyond above" (Ephesians 1:21).

The glory of God in Christ is beyond our full comprehension. Paul describes the glory of God in Christ as being above all rule, authority, power, and lordship in time and eternity. Paul refers to "the Father of glory" (Ephesians 1:17) and the Father of glory has seated Christ with Him (Ephesians 1:20). The glory of God should be the supreme notion of all Christians. The *Westminster Shorter Catechism* asserts that the chief end of man is to glorify God and the Bible proves it. "And He (God) put all things under His (Christ) feet, and gave Him (Christ) to be head over all things to the church, which is His (Christ) body, the fullness of Him who fills all in all" (Ephesians 1:22).

The church magnifies and celebrates the glory of God in Christ and humbly receives the blessing of His grace. In our joy or our sadness, in our pleasure or our pain, in the secular or the sacred, the highest object in worship is the glory of God in Christ.

4. The Grace of God for Dead Men

Ephesians 2:1-3

The message of the Bible sums up the condition of natural man: "You being dead in trespasses and sins." Although Paul originally wrote this letter to the Ephesian Church, the application extends to all God's children. Without blushing Paul asserts the former condition for every Christian: "you were dead."

The word dead essentially means without life. It may be used as a metaphor and a figure of speech or refer to a literal physical death. In this case it is a metaphor for the alienation of a favorable relationship with God. To put it another way it was a spiritual death of the soul of man. John Calvin posited, "spiritual death is nothing else than the alienation of the soul from God."

Human beings are physically alive when they are born, but spiritually dead when they come into this world. Therefore the Bible asserts, you were dead in trespasses and sins. Since the New Testament was originally written in the Greek language there is a slight distinction in this text. The Greek text translated word for word: "And you are dead in the trespasses and in the sins." The English translation from the New American Standard Bible: "And you were dead in your trespasses and sins."

There is a rule in Greek grammar known as the Granville Sharp rule. If two nouns are connected by the Greek copulative (conjunction) *kai* (and) and both nouns have a definite article in the same case (the) the second noun compliments the first noun. In this case trespasses and sins are different words, but they complement each other. Trespasses refer to falling away from or moving from God's narrow way to the right or to the left; a deviation from God's straight and narrow path. Paul used the word trespasses in chapter one. "In Him we have redemption through His blood, the forgiveness of trespasses" (Ephesians 1:7).

We are not only dead in trespasses but dead in sins. New Testament scholar, William Hendriksen, states their sins referred to "their inclinations." I can hardly distinguish the two. Without explaining the exact meaning, it seems to me that Paul wants to emphasize the universal scope of the fall of man.

Unfortunately many preachers and theologians speak of man being spiritually sick rather than spiritually dead. The *Westminster Confession of Faith* briefly but thoroughly explains,

> From this original corruption, whereby we are utterly indisposed, disabled, and made opposite to all good, and wholly inclined to all evil, do proceed all actual transgressions. (*Westminster Confession of Faith*, chapter 6, section 4)

Man by his fall into a state of sin lost all ability to any spiritual good.

Why would Paul speak to the church at Ephesus about such an unpopular doctrine? Ephesus was a pig pen of sin. From the way Paul describes Ephesus in the Book of Acts, the people of that fair city were certainly idolaters. If they loved and served pagan idols, then there were probably adulterers, drunks, thieves, and liars as well.

Ephesus was like any other city in the United States, a secular city. The people walked around but they were actually dead; that is dead in trespasses and sins. Paul described the exercise of their sin in terms of:

> You once walked according to the course of this world

Ephesians

You once walked according to the prince of the power of the air

There was a time when all Christians walked with the environment of which they loved and cherished. There was a time when the spirit of Satan controlled their lives. They gladly walked according to His principles.

It is Satan, by means of a spiritual demonic world, who engages the wicked person to more evil by deception. The Bible posits you are dead in trespasses and sins, which is a very serious matter. I remember one church elder saying, "death is always serious."

The Dutch theologian, Louis Berkhof, said that Augustine meant that "the sinful state and condition in which man is born by nature form part of the penalty of sin." The phrase "born by nature" refers to the imputation of sin. Total depravity, original sin, and imputed guilt are not popular doctrines in most professing evangelical churches. Imputed guilt requires further explanation.

> The first human, Adam, acted as the federal head or the legal representative for the entire human race. (This is the root of covenant theology.) The concept of federal theology is profoundly biblical. The inspired apostle Paul makes it very clear that "through one man's offense [Adam's sin] judgment came to all men, resulting in condemnation . . ." (Romans 5:18). The imputation [legal representation] of Adam's sin is often misunderstood. Please notice "the guilt" of Adam's sin was imputed, not the sin itself. Francis Turretin gives a clear and brief, but definitive statement on guilt. Turretin said, "Guilt is the obligation to punishment from previous sin" (*Institutes of Elenctic Theology*, Francis Turretin, vol. 1, p. 594). Adam's sin was sufficient to require the condemnation of the entire

human race. This doctrine tells us that God's justice is absolute. Christ redeemed those whom God calls to Himself, which tells us that God's love is arbitrary. God demands justice in His covenant relationship with the human race, but He demonstrates mercy to His people even though they are covenant breakers. The corruption conveyed to the human race refers to the moral pollution, which remains throughout this life. The grace of justification removes the guilt and the work of sanctification washes away the moral pollution by the most powerful work of the Holy Spirit. (*The Doctrine of Sound Words*, by Martin Murphy).

Our bodies are very much alive in this world, but because of sin the unregenerate, unjustified man is very dead in his relationship with God. In the same manner a dead soul is very much alive to evil. When we speak of a dead soul, we are speaking about an irreparable estrangement of the soul from God. When the wrath of God falls on the sons of disobedience they walk (live) according to the course of this world, according to the prince of the power of the air.

Paul describes himself as one who once lived in the lusts of the flesh. The sinful nature was not only imputed, but Paul concludes that Christians conducted themselves in the lusts of the flesh. To put it another way they actively participated in a sinful lifestyle. The sin nature gives way to the will of the flesh. The soul makes a conscious decision to live according to the Flesh. The flesh describes all the sensible desires and all the passions that Christians experience because of their corrupt nature.

The soul also accommodates the will of the mind. The mind refers to the intellect, correct thinking, and truth. "And you, who once were alienated and enemies in your mind by wicked works" (Colossians 1:21).The distinction between the flesh, will and the mind does not separate their essential unity.

Paul explains professing Christians "were once children of wrath." They were filled with anger. Their passions were out of control. Their lives were mass confusion.

If you think you are dead in trespasses and sin throw yourself on the mercy of God and seek the Lord while He may be found.

5. The Grace of God's Love

Ephesians 2:4-7

The splendor of God's grace shines "because of His great love" for the church. Professing Christians will not understand or experience the grandeur of His love for the church until they grasp the meaning of, "You who were dead in trespasses and sins."

- You once walked according to the course of this world.
- You once walked according to the prince of the power of the air.
- You once lived in the lusts of the flesh.
- You once lived by the desires of your understanding.

God is merciful and loves His children even when they were dead in trespasses and sin. Is it possible to make any sense out of God's grace if He is perfect in every way and all human beings were dead in trespasses and sin? Yes it is. God is independent. He can demonstrate His mercy by His grace. Sinners who were dead in trespasses and sin are dependent.

> They depend on God for everything.
> They depend on God for His covenant promise.
> They depend on God for wisdom and knowledge.

Christians understand and recognize God's grace by their total dependence on Him. Many preachers have failed to preach and teach the theology of God's independence. They have taught a moralistic view of man's perceived independence rather than man's dependence on God because of his sinful condition. The failure to recognize man's dependent and sinful condition leads him to believe he can do something about his sin nature. If this doctrine is taken to its logical end the sinner thinks he can save himself. A misunderstanding of man's sinful condition will naturally and logically lead to a misunderstanding of God's mercy and love.

Mercy and love are certainly inseparably connected, but mercy and love are different. Mercy refers to compassion. Two blind men cried to Jesus, "Have mercy on us" (Matthew 9:27).

The rich man in Hell cried "Father Abraham, have mercy on me" (Luke 16:24). Mercy comes from God freely, without any strings attached. Paul quotes Moses in Exodus where God said to Moses: "I will have mercy on whomever I will have mercy" (Romans 9:15).

Too many generations of professing Christians have been taught that mercy is earned or in most recent times it is said that mercy is an entitlement. That kind of teaching shows a defective view of man's sinful condition. It is needless to pursue any understanding of the Christian doctrine of salvation until Christians understand that human beings are "dead in trespasses and sin." Human beings cannot do anything to obtain salvation, because they are dead in trespasses and sin and God hates sin.

How is it conceivable that God can hate a man who is dead in trespasses and sin and love a man who is dead in trespasses in sin at the same time in the same relationship? I have often heard it said that God loves the sinner, but hates his sin; it is absolutely unbiblical.

Love is a characteristic of God that is found in all His attributes. The *Westminster Shorter Catechism* has a brief definition of God. "God is a Spirit infinite eternal unchangeable in His being wisdom, power, holiness, justice, goodness, and truth." God's love is fundamental to all these attributes and is demonstrated in a special way to His children. For example:

> God's power is directed because of His love.
> God's justice is adjudicated because of His love.
> God's truth is made known because of His love.

It has been said, "Christians must presuppose God's love to understand his character." God's love is always free of prejudice. With His last breath, Jesus prayed for those who murdered Him. The Bible abundantly teaches God's love is a loving rebuke and correction (Matthew 5-7).

It takes courage, strength of character, and humility to show love the way God shows His love to His church. There is no justice or truth, if we distort God's love, which is so easy to do since we are sinful creatures. God's love for His church is so great that it cannot be fully comprehended and it cannot be clearly defined in human language. God's love for His church is intense, deeply personal, unique, spontaneous, sovereign, eternal, and infinite. The prophets explained God's saving love.

> "When Israel was a child, I loved, him" (Hosea 11:1).
> "I have loved you with an everlasting love" (Jeremiah 31:3).

The church understands and feels the grace of God's love. In the words of Paul, "God's love is great" (Ephesians 2:4). The Greek word translated great refers to much (much more) or specifically "the quality of the many." Notice the grammar in the phrase "God loved us." It sounds like a past tense, but the word "loved" is an aorist verb in the Greek text, which means the action has no limits. God's great love was demonstrated by the death of Jesus Christ on the cross for the sake of the true church. Jesus did not die for the righteous, for the good ole boys, for church members or for the poor or the rich. Jesus Christ died for the elect even while they were dead in trespasses. In this context, His elect is a synonym for His church. God made His church alive together with Christ when they were dead in trespasses. His grace is a glorious thought because of His glorious love.

Being made alive in Christ has benefits you cannot imagine. Resurrection and rest are the keywords for the person whom God has made alive in Christ. This resurrection and rest is not explicitly reserved for the life to come. It describes our spiritual state now. The effects of being made alive in Christ are evident by a new mind, emotions and will. As Professor Gordon Clarke said, "we have new ideas, new convictions, and new desires."

Questions we should all ask:

1. Do you understand the love of God in light of your sinfulness? Have you experienced the glory of God's love in your new birth?

2. Have you been raised up together with Christ?

3. Are you resting in Christ, so that your life is one great big huge worship experience?

If you cannot answer yes to those questions, then perhaps you need to go back and read the previous chapter on "The Grace of God for Dead Men" and pray for God to have mercy on your soul. If you can answer yes to those questions, then you may continue to see the "exceeding riches of God's grace in His kindness toward you in Christ Jesus."

6. The Grace of God's Saving Faith

Ephesians 2:8-10

The subject in the letter to the Ephesians is God, more specifically the Grace of God.

Most preaching and teaching today focuses on human beings and all their alleged needs; however, after listening to most preachers, it is prosperity for the body. Listen to Christian radio and T. V. and you will quickly discover that the emphasis in sermons, teaching and music is on human beings. Church leaders design worship services to entertain folks by creating fuzzy psychological feelings that in turn create big bank accounts.

Christians must be awakened. Clean breaks with the past are absolutely necessary for the preservation of the church. Many preachers don't want to hear about the state of the church in North America, because it's gloom and doom. Reason for these gloom and doom prognostications is that it is obvious that the society and culture we once knew as Christians is quickly disappearing. Orthodox doctrine like justification by faith alone is buried under a mountain of false doctrine.

The Bible teaches sinners cannot do anything to be saved, not even exercise their faith, because it's not their faith. Faith is a gift of God. It should not surprise professing Christians that God gives faith as a gift. All of creation is a gift. It's all about God's grace.

God gives sinners the gift of faith because they were dead in trespasses, but by God's grace they were made alive (Ephesians 2:5). Unfortunately, the modern church has taught that salvation depends on what sinners do. Every world religion lays emphasis on self-effort or doing something to gain eternal salvation.

Yet Christianity is the only religion in the world that believes and teaches that eternal salvation is absolutely a gift of God, from beginning to end.

If *your* faith is the instrument of salvation, then you have done something to create faith. The Bible states the correct doctrine: "faith is not of works, lest anyone should boast" (Ephesians 2:9). The sin nature wants to work for eternal salvation. Even after God gives new life, faith, and sanctification, the sin nature still wants to work for salvation.

The righteousness of Christ does not need to work to be saved. The righteousness of Christ wants to work for the glory of God's love. It is incongruous to Scripture and sound reason that God does one thing such as give grace and then the human being does something else to earn eternal salvation.

Professing Christians ought to be deeply disturbed about the false teaching in the church today. Some Christians may have heard and perhaps adopted into their world view in years past a quasi-grace doctrine. The church should be reformed by the Word of God.

I hope you will ask yourself the question: What are my children learning today? What will my grandchildren learn in the generation to come? The Word of God has a warning for the church.

> And the Lord said to me, The prophets prophesy lies in My name. I have not sent them, commanded them, nor spoken to them; they prophesy to you a false vision, divination, a worthless thing and the deceit of their heart. (Jeremiah 14:14)

A few years ago a newspaper reported that the largest Presbyterian denomination in the United States, represented by its leaders, "agreed to amend their constitution to support fidelity in all relationships of life" in an attempt to temper a rule that bars homosexuals from the pulpit.

How did it come to this? Many generations ago those congregations were told salvation was a result of their good works (not in so many words, but that is what was communicated).

It was the deceit in the hearts of the prophets (the elders in the church, both ruling and teaching) that has brought many a church down this disgusting road to apostasy. The church has not been taught as Scripture so clearly teaches that "we are His workmanship." God created His church, adds to the church each day and provides for it.

The elect are the product of God's grace created in Christ Jesus for good works. God saved His church for good works. God predestined our good works in Christ, not for the purpose of salvation, but for the glory of God. Therefore, salvation of the elect is the glory of God's grace.

7. The Grace of God in the Blood of Christ

Ephesians 2:11-13

Paul warns the Ephesian Church to remember their past. The same warning applies to the contemporary church. God is glorified when the church remembers what He has done for the church. When Christians arrive at that place of success or they have lived a long life of relatively good times, they too often forget that God is the one who caused it all. A professing Christian may say, I've got a nice home, a nice car, a nice truck, a nice tract of land, a nice boat, or a nice bank account, but actually Christians do not own any of those things.

The church at Ephesus like professing Christians of all times at all places are commanded to remember the time when they did not have what they have now, namely salvation by grace through faith.

God had not demonstrated his saving grace.
God had not given them the gift of faith.

The truth is, "you who once were far off have been brought near by the blood of Christ" (Ephesians 2:13). Christians will remember the grace of God in the blood of Christ.

Paul uses the ethnic and religious background of the Jews and the Gentiles to get the attention of the church at Ephesus. The Jews were a proud people, because they were known as the people of God. They were God's Chosen People.

The Jews used pejorative terms to describe Gentiles as anyone who was not a Jew. The Bible explains, "you, once

Gentiles in the flesh who were called uncircumcision by what is called the circumcision made in the flesh by hand." Uncircumcision referred to the disenfranchisement from the people of God. The Circumcision often referred to the covenant people of God, but notice how Paul refers to them in this text. They are the Circumcision made "in the flesh" by hands. "In the flesh" could refer to that which glorified God or that which God hated.

This terminology is found very early in the Bible. "And you shall be circumcised in the flesh of your foreskin; And it shall be the sign of the covenant between Me and you" (Genesis 17:11). "In the flesh" was the outward mark of God's covenant with His people. There are times when "in the flesh" refers to immoral sinister practices. For example, Ezekiel prophesied,

> Thus says the Lord God: O house of Israel, let us have no more of your abominations. When you brought in foreigners, uncircumcised in heart and uncircumcised in flesh, to be in My sanctuary to defile it... .(Ezekiel 44:6)

The term "in the flesh" may be good and godly on one hand, but evil and sinister on the other.

Paul reminds the Ephesian Gentiles of their former condition before they were brought near the kingdom of God. Paul also wants to remind the Jewish Christians that carnal circumcision (that is, made by hands) means nothing.

In the same way baptism means nothing if it is merely an outward sign. An outward mark without an inward change is carnal and worthless. However, the emphasis is on the fact that the Gentiles were dead in their trespasses and sins.

The message to the human race is, "without Christ, being aliens from the commonwealth of Israel and strangers from the covenants of promise, having no hope and without God in the world" (Ephesians 2:12). That verse describes the utter despair of the human race after the fall of man. The *Westminster Shorter Catechism* discusses Adam being good before the Fall, but bad after the Fall because of sin. The first mark of the human race after the fall of man is "without God in the world." The word is atheism. The second mark of the human race after the fall of man is "having no hope."

The word hope in the New Testament has a decidedly different meaning than the mundane use of the word hope. New Testament biblical hope is objective. Secular hope is subjective. There are three factors that give hope its meaning in the New Testament. Hope is not ego-centric. It is Christ centered and glorifies God. "Let us be sober having put on the breastplate of faith and love, and as a helmet, the hope of salvation" (1 Thessalonians 5:8). Hope does not rest on good works, but rests on the gracious work of God in Jesus Christ. "Paul, an apostle of Christ Jesus according to the commandment of God our Savior, and of Christ Jesus, who is our hope" (1 Timothy 1:1). Hope is like faith in that it is a gift from God.

> Now may our Lord Jesus Christ Himself and God our Father, who has loved us and given us eternal comfort and good hope by grace comfort and strengthen your hearts in every good work and word. (2 Thessalonians 2:16)

The third mark of the human race after the fall is loneliness. Paul's language is, "strangers from the covenants of promise." Biblical covenants in the Old Testament are fulfilled in this promise: the saving work of Christ as prophet, priest, and king.

The fourth mark of the human race after the fall is their disenfranchisement from orderly government as the Bible posits, "being aliens from the commonwealth of Israel."

The fifth mark of the human race after the fall is that they are without Christ.

This portion of God's Word raises a question. How can man be without Christ if God choose the elect before the foundation of the world? Prior to conversion man had not experienced what it means to be "in Christ." Man had not seen the glory of God. God is glorified by the blood of Christ, because He removed the guilt of sin which man could not remove.

Christ humiliated Himself by taking on the form of human nature, living a sinless life, completely fulfilling God's law, suffering for the sake of His church, and dying the horrible death on the cross all for the glory of God.

The term propitiation is relative to this discussion. Propitiation comes from an Old Testament practice. The high priest would enter the holy of holies to sprinkle the ark of the Lord with the atoning blood of the lamb. Propitiation refers to the satisfaction of divine justice. Jesus Christ satisfied God's divine wrath against His elect. Propitiation is connected with the doctrines of forgiveness, mercy, grace, and reconciliation. Christ and His shed blood is our propitiation. Christ propitiated or turned away the wrath of God by offering Himself in our place.

Some theologians argue that the word expiation best describes Christ's atoning work. The problem is that expiation refers to the cancellation of sin rather than the turning away of God's wrath. Rome uses the expiation concept to explain how men are purged of their sins. The blood of Christ did not purge me of my sins. The blood of Christ covers my sin and sins so that God does not condemn me for my sin or sins.

> For such a High Priest was fitting for us, who is holy, harmless, undefiled, separate from sinners, and has become higher than the heavens; who does not need daily, as those high priests, to offer up sacrifices, first

for His own sins and then for the people's for this He did once for all when He offered up Himself. (Hebrews 7:26-27)

The grace of God in the blood of Christ is the doctrine that brings to the forefront the sinners understanding of their spiritual union with Jesus Christ.

8. The Grace of God's Peace

Ephesians 2:14-22

The glory of God is the purpose of true worship. The church glorifies God when His people recognize and worship Him reasonably and sensibly. God's glory and worship is the pinnacle of Christianity.

Worship touches the soul because it has a theological basis. Theological worship exalts God's nature and character. Sometimes it requires the church to believe the unbelievable, because God is metaphysical. For instance, "God chose us in Christ before the foundation of the world" is a theological expression (Ephesians 1:4).

The church worships aesthetically. To put it another way, the church must understand the beauty of God in His excellent holiness, even though it is challenging to believe His plan for the church. "In Him also we have obtained an inheritance being predestined according to the purpose of Him who works all things according to the counsel of His will" (Ephesians 1:11).

Epistemology is the science or study of knowledge. It answers the question: How do we know what we know? The theory of knowledge is essential for theological inquiry. Therefore, we must know who and how to worship. It is necessary to understand God intelligently. "Paul prayed that the God of our Lord Jesus Christ, the Father of glory, may give to you the spirit of wisdom and revelation in the knowledge of Him, the eyes of your understanding being enlightened" (Ephesians 1:17-18).

To worship emotionally means the church must understand God affectionately. There is an emotional expression during worship if your relationship with God is peace. For He Himself is our peace" (Ephesians 2:14).

Christians will never understand peace with God unless they understand their broken relationship with God. Paul referred to it as, "dead in trespasses and sins" (Ephesians 2:1). The only hope of reconciliation between God and man is for someone to satisfy God's wrath. The sacrifice of Jesus Christ was the sacrifice that satisfied God's wrath. Christ was not only our peacemaker, He is our peace. The word peace may refer to one's well-being, good health, or it may refer to the absence of war.

When Paul used the word "peace" in the letter to the Ephesians, I believe he had the comprehensive full orbed view of peace in mind. The Word of God must be considered in its fullness, so there is a portion of God's word that says there is no peace. God warned His people during a time they rebelled against God: "For they [prophets and priests] have healed the hurt of the daughter of My people slightly, saying, 'Peace, peace!' when there is no peace" (Jeremiah 8:10). The religious leaders in Israel like the religious leaders in the contemporary Christian church offers "slight" relief to the people living in confusion and distress. Slight healing is nothing more than false healing. Sin is no longer called death, it is merely sickness. External religion is the popular image that produces sensational feelings. There are two kinds of peace; one is true and the other is false.

On another occasion God promised peace.

> "And He shall stand and feed His flock in the strength of the Lord, in the majesty of the name of the Lord His God; And they shall abide, for now He shall be great to the ends of the earth; And this One shall be peace." (Micah 5:4-5)

The capstone to understanding the doctrine of peace is

found in Paul's letter to the Romans. "Therefore, having been justified by faith, we have peace with God through our Lord Jesus Christ...(Romans 5:1). Very simple. Without Christ no peace. With Christ one shares in the peace of Christ

The church should assemble peaceably because as members of the body of Christ they want to worship and glorify Christ as the object of their peace. Apparently the Jewish and Gentile Christians at Ephesus fought among themselves. The Jew, no doubt, said that his circumcision and his law made him a privileged Christian. However, Paul reminded the Gentiles of their past when they were marked by their:

1. atheism - without God
2. hopelessness - having no hope
3. loneliness - strangers from the covenants of promise
4. disenfranchised from orderly government
5. being aliens from the commonwealth of Israel
6. they were without Christ

A rather dismal situation living a gloomy and unpleasant life. There was a barrier between God and man. Christ broke the barrier for both Jew and Gentile, as Scripture says he has made both one. Oneness is an important concept. By nature God created Adam a helpmeet because man should not be separated. Adam and Eve lived in peace before they sinned against God. It is unnatural to have division, strife, and dissension. God's plan was for order and harmony, not equality and strife. In the beginning there were no Jews and Gentiles. The fallen nature provided the catalyst to divide into Jew and Gentile and so forth.

Christ broke the barrier between God and man by breaking the middle wall of partition as a symbol of His reconciliation. This may be a reference to the temple where a wall separated the Jews from the Gentiles. Christ broke the barrier between

God and man by abolishing the ceremonial laws and replacing them with the once for all sacrifice of His only Son, our Lord Jesus Christ.

Christ became peace for the church so that He might create from all people - one people - without hostility, dissension, and division. Christ died to put hostility, dissension and division to death. Christ not only died and was resurrected to bring peace; He made a public proclamation of His peace. "And He came and preached peace to you who were afar off and to those who were near" (Ephesians 2:17). He preached peace to those far away and near the kingdom of God.

Whether you were far away or near, it is the same Spirit that causes the new birth in Jesus Christ and supplies the peace of Christ. These two simple truths take strangers and turn them in fellow citizens. Jews and Gentiles are fellow citizens in the kingdom of God. Citizenship is an important concept, because citizenship presumes allegiance as a citizen to the government that has given the privilege of citizenship. Christians are living a sacred life in a secular world. Christians are living a sacred life in a sojourners world. Christians uniquely have "citizenship in heaven" (Philippians 3:20). However, Christians "conduct yourselves in a manner worthy of the gospel of Christ" (Philippians 1:27). The word "conduct" comes from the same root word in which we find the word citizen in the Ephesian text (Ephesians 2:19). The word conduct has to do with "how to live as a citizen." Christians are living like citizens of heaven, but they live in a secular or what I call a sojourners world. Christians live in this world for a short time, but they are actually citizens of another world. The apostle Peter posits we are aliens and sojourners in this world (1 Peter 2:11).

Your first birth, your physical birth, made you a citizen on this earth, let's say of the USA. However, Your spiritual birth made you a citizen of heaven. A description of the sacred life is that of a person who has the blessing of this dual citizenship. Christians should anticipate the land of their citizenship, the New Heavens and New Earth.

There are no distinctions in the land of our eternal citizenship. In contrast, Paul likened the Gentiles to individual nomads traveling from one place to the other and never having any permanent family ties. Now they are members of the family of God.

The peace that Christians claim in Christ is comprehensive. Christian believers have the kind of peace that is full and complete. They are no longer at war with God. They are no longer at war with each other.

The peace of Christ has brought a complete and full relationship between God and man. If you do not have that complete and full relationship then I urge you to cast yourself upon God for His grace and mercy. The peace of Christ also heals relationships among believers. The peace of Christ brings wholeness to our understanding of God and fellow Christians. "And let the peace of God rule in your hearts, to which also you were called in one body; and be thankful" (Colossians 3:15).

9. The Grace of God's Revelation of Christ

Ephesians 3:1-7

About the time Jesus Christ died on the cross, a man named Ignatius was born. He became a Christian and died a martyr's death around 107 A.D. for his Christian beliefs.

On the way to Rome and the martyr's death, he wrote a letter to the Ephesian church commending, encouraging and challenging them to stand firm in the faith. At one point in his letter he asked the question:

> Why do we not, as gifted with reason, act wisely?" He went on to ask: "Why do we fall headlong into ignorance?" After asking those most poignant questions he urged them saying: "Be ye therefore the ministers of God and the mouth of Christ." "Everyone that has received from God the power of distinguishing and yet follows an unskillful shepherd, and receives a false opinion for the truth, shall be punished. What communion hath truth with falsehood?" (*Ante Nicene Fathers*, vol. 1, p. 49-58)

As a minister of the gospel Ignatius was concerned that the church at Ephesus might ignore the revelation of Jesus Christ. The revelation of Christ is central to the Christian religion; therefore, revelation is necessary for the church. Every Christian preacher or teacher should be concerned that the glory of God in the revelation of Jesus Christ may be trampled by the modern church.

The professing Christians at Ephesus apparently had not taken seriously the revelation given to them by those who preached at Ephesus, beginning with Paul. They had abused the gift of revelation and the glory that accompanies it. The church must consider and reconsider the glory of God in the revelation of Jesus Christ.

Revelation in this text means something had been hidden but is now revealed; something is unveiled. Before it was revealed it was a mystery. The mystery of Christ had been revealed to the Gentiles at Ephesus. Prior to the revelation of Christ, the only revelation they had was the revelation of the wrath of God.

The power of the Holy Spirit changed their hearts and they were made worthy to receive the revelation of Christ. The gospel was revealed and the grace of God given as a gift to the sinner. Why can't unbelievers see the truth of God's saving grace? They can't see because the gospel is a secret. It is an eternal secret. "The secret things belong to the Lord our God, but those things which are revealed belong to us and to our children forever..." (Deuteronomy 29:29). Sometimes God limits His revelation for the good of His people. However, if God plainly reveals something to His church, God's people must not ignore it.

So how does the Lord reveal Himself? The Bible answers: "Which in other ages was not made known to the sons of men, as it has now been revealed by the Spirit to His holy apostles and prophets" (Ephesians 3:5). The revealed secret or unveiled mystery is a work of God and He doesn't work to reveal anything apart from his Word. Children of Satan do not understand the revelation of God's Word, because the Holy Spirit has not enabled them to believe (John 8:47). "Surely the Lord God does nothing, unless He reveals His secret counsel to His servants the prophets" (Amos 3:7). The child of God must read God's Word to understand the mystery of Christ.

The mystery Paul revealed to the Ephesian church also applies to the contemporary church. The Gentiles were gathered into the church the same way as the Jews. Paul explains, "That the Gentiles should be fellow heirs. Of the same body and partakers of His promise in Christ through the gospel..." (Ephesians 3:6).

Contrary to true revelation, there is false revelation. Paul speaks of the revelation "made known to him" (Ephesians 3:3). I think Paul was concerned about the false apostles of his day boasting about their own revelations. The Book of Acts records the last account of Paul meeting with the elders of the Ephesian Church. Paul warned them of false teachers infiltrating the church.

> Paul's greatest concern was the danger of heresy and false teachers. Paul called them savage wolves and warned the Ephesian elders that they would "draw away the disciples after themselves" (Acts 20:30). Savage wolves will infiltrate the ranks of the church. The savage wolves will introduce false doctrine. Like their father the Devil, the savage wolves will try to mislead the disciples of Christ with false preaching and teaching. Jesus warned the disciples to "Beware of false prophets, who come to you in sheep's clothing, but inwardly they are ravenous wolves" (Matthew 7:15). Savage ravenous wolves may come in the form of celebrated religious leaders. (*The Church: First Thirty Years*, by Martin Murphy, p.256)

Jesus warned the church to,

> Beware of the scribes, who desire to go around in long robes, love greetings in the marketplaces, the best seats in the synagogues, and the best places at feasts, who

devour widows' houses, and for a pretense make long prayers. (Mark.12:38)

Jesus also left the church these words of warning, "Beware of the leaven of the Pharisees, which is hypocrisy" (Luke. 12:1).

False revelation is hypocrisy, playacting or may be best described as pretending. The two Greek words translated hypocrisy literally refers to "not making a good judgment." Today there are many false teachers who brag on their own revelations. When Christians judge wrongly about the revelation of Jesus Christ, they are not acting wisely, but are "falling headlong into ignorance" as Ignatius would say.

Remember what Ignatius said to the Ephesian Church: "Everyone that has received from God the power of distinguishing and yet follows an unskillful shepherd, and receives a false opinion (that is a heresy), shall be punished." The world of electronic communication, Radio, TV, Internet, and the publishing industry abounds with false teachers announcing new revelation (often old revelation in new clothes). The piercing question: how much of it is true? How much of it rests upon the special revelation of Jesus Christ?

The only way to maintain sanity in this pluralist world is to bring "every thought into captivity to the obedience of Christ." New believers may be challenged to a new understanding of biblical doctrine. Sometimes understanding the Word of God slowly progresses. God does not give to all in all ages the same measure of light.

For example, the revelation of the Messiah was revealed by degrees to Old Testament saints; Adam, Noah, Abraham, Moses, David, and Jeremiah. In any case the revelation must be progressive to one degree or another. How foolish are those who will believe no more than their fathers. Each generation must be reformed by the Word of God. When Joash became King of Judah the Bible says he "did what was right in the sight of the Lord all the days of Jehoiada the priest" (2

Chronicles 24:2). When Joash's son, Amaziah, became king the Bible says he "did right in the sight of the Lord, yet not with a whole heart" (2 Chronicles 25:2). When Amaziah's son, Uzziah, became king the Bible says he did right in the sight of the Lord according to all that his father Amaziah had done" (2 Chronicles 26:4). When Uzziah's son, Jotham, became king the Bible says he "did right in the sight of the Lord according to all that his father Uzziah had done; however he did not enter the temple of the Lord." In the same way each generation in Judah fell away from the revelation that was originally given, so has the church over the past generations.

The orthodox doctrine of the church revealed in Scripture is being replaced with trendy ways of ministry and worship. Man-made tradition applied to worship is unacceptable. Only heavenly revelation that directs the church how to worship God is acceptable. Man-made doctrine is unacceptable.

The gospel is a sacred trust. The church has the solemn duty to pass on the doctrine explaining the gift of the grace of God to the coming generations, pure and undefiled, so that God is glorified in the revelation of Jesus Christ.

10. The Grace of God in the Mystery of Christ

Ephesians. 3:8-13

It is a challenge to understand Paul's long Greek sentences translated into English. However, the perspicuity of Scripture is available to the believer who searches for the truth of the gospel. Another challenge is translating Greek words into English. For instance, Paul affirms, "I was made a minister...to preach to the Gentiles" (Ephesians 3:7-8). God called Paul to be a minister for the purpose of preaching the unsearchable riches of Christ.

The definition of the word "minister" needs some explanation because Christians attach so much cultural baggage to many of the words used in religious discussions. In this context Paul chose the Greek word *diakinos* to describe himself as a minister. The Greek word *diakonos* is translated into English as deacon, servant, and minister. It essentially means to serve.

Paul speaks of himself as a servant of Christ (1 Corinthians 4:1), so without question the minister or the servant serves God according to God's call so that God's children (God's flock) receives the benefit of the minister's call. God's minister has been called for the good of the congregation.

The Bible posits, "For he is God's minister to you for good" (Romans 13:4). Minister refers to the civil authority or the ruler. The early English Puritans referred to him as the civil magistrate. We refer to the civil magistrate in terms of "the government." The government is God's minister to you for good. If the government is acting in an evil manner toward you, is he still your minister? Not according to God's Word. If I act in an evil manner, I'm not God's servant. A minister as we find the word in our text refers to someone who serves others for the benefit and good of the one being served.

The church today seems to be held in disdain by the majority of the world. It is the result of ministers who do not understand what it means to be a minister. Some people view a minister as ignorant, lazy, and fat - maybe not in that order and maybe not all three, but some combination of the three to some degree or the other. Unquestionably the minister, more often than not, is debased if not literally despised.

I would have to agree that many ministers are lazy and many are them do not appear to be endowed with gifts for ministry. Some ministers are bright and industrious, but too often their efforts appear to be self-seeking and egotistic. So there is a sense in which the minister has caused a cloud to come over the ministry of the church.

However, the Apostle still seems to make much to do over the fact that he is a minister.

> Ephesians 3:7 - "I became a minister"
> Colossians 1:25 - "I became a minister"

The Apostle Paul viewed himself as one who had been called by the effective working of God's power. He was called to minister to God's people. The question is this: how did he minister to God's people? First, he ministered in His apostolic office. God revealed the eternal Word of God by making known the mystery of Christ. Secondly, he ministered to God's people by preaching to them. The inspired Apostle didn't believe that preaching was a matter of using eloquent persuasive words of human wisdom, but rather preaching is the demonstration of the Spirit and power of God. You may differ with the apostle, but before you do let me remind you from the Word of God that preaching is saving to some and

Ephesians

damning to others. No one can escape the effect of preaching if it is truly preaching. The verity of efficacious preaching is found in 2 Corinthians 2:12-17. Paul the minister declared, "For we are not, as so many, peddling the word of God" (2 Corinthians 2:17).

The call to minister the gospel through the preaching of the Word of God is a sober, grave, serious, potent, and life threatening call. Study 2 Corinthians 2:12-17, James 3:1, Ezekiel 33:1-10. Paul declared to the Ephesian church, "To me, who am less than the least of all the saints, this grace was given, that I should preach among the Gentiles the unsearchable riches of Christ" (Ephesians 3:8).

What was unsearchable? The word unsearchable derives from two Greek words literally meaning "not able to trace out." The word is found one other place in the New Testament. "Oh, the depth of the riches both of the wisdom and knowledge of God! How unsearchable are His judgments and His ways past finding out" (Romans 11:33). Some preachers may use this text to prove that God is unknowable and so they place little effort in preaching. They fail to do the hard job of preaching on the nature and character of God. The unsearchable riches are "both of the wisdom and knowledge of God."

Paul told the Ephesians that the manifold wisdom of God should be made known by the church. God's manifold wisdom refers to the many different aspects of God's wisdom. The wisdom of God is infinite. God will always choose good and His means are appropriate to His character. God's ways are sadly misunderstood because of the sin nature, yet all His wisdom reflected in His providence should be the objects of awe and admiration. If people are offended by God's inscrutable will (unsearchable will), they are charting a course without the wisdom of God. The complexity of circumstances in this day and age must not cause Christians to question God's goodness and care. It is our simple feeble sinful wisdom that we should despise. If we ask why God allowed such and such to happen, it is an offense to God that we would question his goodness and wisdom. God's unsearchable wisdom must not be a stumbling block. The unsearchable riches of Christ give Christians the wisdom they need. The Bible posits that the fear of the Lord is wisdom (Job 28:28). Wisdom is associated with two dimensions of existence: the empirical (experience) and the rational (intellect).

Christians should have an interest in the affairs of this world such as moral and ethical applications, economic theories, political life, education, civil and social concerns. The unsearchable riches of Christ include the mundane physical life, but the primary concern is the eternal and metaphysical relation with the triune God.

> When we ask questions like:
> What is life all about?
> Why am I here or why do I exist?
> Is there a God and what is God like?
> What is God doing about the mess in this world?

We are asking questions that if answered to any degree requires wisdom; if we do not use wisdom the answers are nonsense.

The unsearchable riches of Christ generously remind professing Christians of their sins, of the sin of their Father Adam, and therefore their need for justification. Christ graciously reminds the sinner of his agony and pain and at the same time reminds the sinner of his need for a Savior. The unsearchable riches of Christ provide the riches of pardon and forgiveness. Some professing Christians do not understand the fullness of God's pardon and forgiveness, but they may have full assurance accompanying the promise of eternal life. Hidden in the unsearchable riches of Christ is:

1) comfort for all those who mourn
2) filling for those who hunger and thirst for righteousness
3) the kingdom of God for those who are persecuted for righteousness sake

The unsearchable riches of Christ are a rich source of peace, for the Apostle himself said, "we have peace with God through the Lord Jesus Christ." The unsearchable riches of Christ gives the church rest. Christ says, "come to me all you who labor and are heavy laden, and I will give you rest" (Matthew 11:28). Christ will give the church rest from the anxieties of this world (a moment by moment turning to Christ). Also, eternal rest.

It is the unsearchable riches of Christ that produces the fruit of the Spirit; love, joy, peace, long-suffering, kindness, goodness, faithfulness, gentleness, and self-control. The unsearchable riches of Christ glorify God.

The Bible does not tell God's people not to search for the riches of Jesus Christ. However, they must search within the limits of God's revelation. The unsearchable riches of Christ may not be fully known, but certainly the riches of Christ are searchable to some extent. The word unsearchable does not mean these valuable riches cannot be known: it means that Christians can't know the full glory of those unsearchable riches.

Do you see the value of these unsearchable riches?

Do you see the abundance of these unsearchable riches?

Do you meditate and think about the unsearchable riches of Christ?

Does the mention of the unsearchable riches of Christ excite you?

Does your spiritual appetite grow each day to search for the unsearchable riches of Christ?

What are you thinking this very moment? It is about the unsearchable riches of Christ.

What appeals to you? The world and all its allurements or the unsearchable riches of Christ.

11. The Grace of God for the Soul of Man

Ephesians 3:14-21

The inspired Apostle Paul has concluded that he must pray for the saints at Ephesus. This is a dramatic juncture. It is not unusual for Paul to pray, but here he bends his knees in prayer. This is not the only place that the Apostle kneels to pray, but that was not necessarily the general posture for prayer. Kneeling was used in very solemn settings. Jesus taught His disciples saying; "whenever you stand praying, if you have anything against anyone, forgive him" (Mark 11:25). Although Jesus prayed at Gethsemane on His knees, Paul's posture in prayer marks his attitude toward God and the seriousness of the occasion.

Paul had a pastoral interest in the Christians at Ephesus and he wanted the congregation to know that he had their best interest at heart. One of the marks of a good pastor is that he will show a genuine interest in the souls of those to whom God has charged him. It is a great challenge and awesome responsibility.

Unfortunately many church members are not interested in their own soul, so the pastor has a tough job. Prayer may become a difficult private task, rather than bringing the joy it should bring as two people, or more than two people, agree on an intercession to God.

Paul's prayer must be understood in the context of his letter to Ephesians. The Apostle has made much to do over the Gentiles coming into the kingdom of God just as the Jews come into the kingdom. The mystery of salvation reveals the glorious revelation of Jesus Christ to Jews and Gentiles. The Jew and Gentile inherit the unsearchable riches of Christ, because God has ordained it. If God ordained it, why should Paul or anyone else pray? It is not merely to express human responsibility. Prayer is an expression of your total dependence on an independent Being.

In Paul's prayer, what does he specifically pray for? What does Paul hope will result from his prayer? Many pastors find this prayer of the Apostle Paul their model prayer for their congregation. I hope elders will adopt this as their model prayer. I hope church members will adopt this prayer as they pray for one another.

The first thing Paul prays for is the congregation at Ephesus might be strengthened. To better understand Paul's prayer, consider two popular Bible translations:

NKJV - "that **he would** grant you"
NIV - "**he may** strengthen you"

"To be strengthened by might" is interesting because the Greek text could literally be translated "to become mighty by power." Christians should ask why do we need to be strengthened or more importantly where do we need strengthened? Paul answers that question at the end of verse 16; we need strength in the inner man. The inner man refers to the spiritual dimension of Christians. Some call it the soul. To compare and contrast:

>The outward man refers to the physical world.
>The inner man refers to the metaphysical being.

The concept of the inner spiritual man was a matter of interest to the early Greek philosophers.

Plato spoke of "the man within" in contrast to the "outward man." One of the most dangerous movements within the church today is the therapeutic movement. The therapist is recognized as one who can solve and heal the psychological aberrations of the human race.

The non-Christian therapist treats the outward man. The Christian therapist treats the inner man.

Both have erred. It is the source of life that fills the soul with life. Without the divine initiative changing the inner man, there will be a rage against reason, morality, and order. The Lord Jesus Christ said, "out of the heart comes evil thoughts, adulteries, fornications, murders', and all such things" (Matthew 15:19).

Christians ought to ask the question "why do we need strength?" Christians (the church) need strength for the soul so they can worship and work according to God's plan and to His glory. The body is temporary. Death is inevitable from the day of birth. The soul is permanent. For the Christian eternal worship in heaven is the reason for existence. While Christians remain in the body, they will struggle with the carnal nature.

Simply put, actual Christians are saved. They believe the promise of eternal salvation and heaven forever. They even have infallible assurance of salvation. But until this body of sin is put to death, sin will visit them until they go to be with the Lord. While they remain on this earth they need an ongoing supply of soul strength with power from the Spirit of God. As Paul says in another place, "Even though our outward man is perishing, yet the inward man is being renewed day by day (2 Corinthians 4:16)."

Unbelievers do not understand the need for this soul strength. They are too worried with the things of this world. Those poor souls know nothing of the need for soul strength. Another reason the soul needs new strength day by day is the weakness of the soul. In his letter to the Corinthian Church the inspired Apostle said, "I could not speak to you as to spiritual people but as to carnal, as to babes in Christ" (1 Corinthians

3:1).

At least some in the Corinthian Church were Christians, but nevertheless weak Christians. It appears that the church at Corinth didn't have godly leadership. The people were not fed with spiritual food, so their souls were weak and sick. Some Christians have been deprived of spiritual food so long, it is impossible for them to take any more than little bites of baby food.

The soul of man also needs to be strengthened because the devil walks around like a roaring lion, seeking whom he may devour. The devil and his angels are deceitful. They appear as angels of light. He can quote Scripture. He is a rational creature, so he can reason with you and give the appearance of presenting truthful arguments. All for the reason of deceiving you and leading you astray.

Only spiritual strength from the Holy Spirit can arm you to resist the devil. Christians recognize the need for spiritual strength. They also recognize they obtain spiritual strength "through His Spirit" (Ephesians 3:16). It is by the power of the Spirit of God that our souls are strengthened, but God is pleased to use instruments to bring this strength to our consciousness. As John Calvin correctly said of this text:

> While the Lord alone acts upon us, he acts by his own instruments. It is therefore the duty of pastors diligently to teach. It is the duty of both (pastors and people) not to weary themselves in unprofitable exertions, but to look up for divine aid.

The Christian mind, emotions, and will are in great need of spiritual strength. The Christian mind needs to understand the truth from God's word. One great sin today is anti-intellectualism. The will needs to be inclined to obey the Word of God. Another great sin today is antinomianism; It describes someone opposed to keeping the law of God.

Emotions (affections) express the godly behavior in real tangible ways. We hope, we love, we rejoice in a godly manner as the expression of our soul strength.

Those are just a few of the many reasons that you should pray to be strengthened by the power of God in the inner man.

Paul's letter to the Ephesians should challenge and encourage Christians to bow their knees to the Father of our Lord Jesus Christ and pray for those who worship the true and living God, as the inspired Apostle says, that Christ may dwell in your hearts through faith. It is true that the natural man does not receive the things of the Spirit of God, for they are foolishness to him, nor can he know them, because they are spiritually discerned.

The outward man glorifies himself. The inner man glorifies Christ. Christ in the heart is the central theme in Paul's prayer. Paul prays purposely that Christ may dwell in the hearts of the Ephesian Christians. Paul wanted the church "to know the love of Christ which passes knowledge" (Ephesians 3:19). Knowledge and love are essential characteristics of Christians. One is not more important than the other. The heart filled with the love of Christ is rooted and grounded in the knowledge of Christ.

Paul ends his prayer with these lovely words from the pastor's heart. He prayed that the church "may be filled with the fullness of God" (Ephesians 3:19). Then Paul praises God with a doxology:

> To Him who is able to do exceedingly abundantly above all that we ask or think, according to the power that works in us, to Him be glory in the church by Christ Jesus to all generations, forever and ever. Amen. (Ephesians 3:20-21)

12. The Grace of God for Your Call

Ephesians 4:1-6

Paul understood his call as a minister of the gospel. Paul said, "I was made a minister" (Ephesians 3:7). It was more than just a designated call for life. This text brings us face to face with the biblical concept often referred to as calling. In *Webster's Encyclopedic Unabridged Dictionary* there are 63 different ways to define the word "call." To properly define the word call you must have a context. The word call, called, or calling is used hundreds of times in the Bible. The primary way the word call is used refers to making a noise to get the attention of someone. When Elijah mocked the false prophets at Mt. Carmel he said, "Call out with a loud voice for he is a god." The Psalmist said, "Answer me when I call O God of my righteousness." Another popular use of the word call or calling is in reference to secular employment. Christians and unbelievers refer to their secular work as a call. It is typical for someone to say, "my calling is to be a merchant, a banker, a clerk, a draftsman, a farmer or any of the other countless professions known to man."

I do not find any direct explicit words in the Bible referring to a secular job as a calling. However, specific words are not necessary to convey an idea or reality, such as secular employment. For example after God created the Garden of Eden the Bible posits, "the Lord God took the man and put him in the garden of Eden to tend and keep it." On the basis of that verse and others, it is the providence of God that brings a person to his secular employment. God did not give a mandate for women having secular employment as a man did, tending and keeping the garden in the perfect world. God did not put Eve in the garden to work it. However, secular employment has pretty well taken over as the primary calling in life, not only for unbelievers, but Christians as well.

There was a time in this country when a man was called to court and marry a girl. It was a call to get married. Callings in the modern and postmodern culture have been and still are maliciously misrepresented by a relativistic society. I expect that is the reason that Webster had to use so much room to define a very simple word.

Paul Helm is teaching fellow at Regent College who wrote a book entitled *The Callings*. He identified four callings:

>God's effective call in conversion
>God's calling in life
>God's call to freedom
>God's heavenly call

The effective call in conversion is the process of someone coming to saving faith in the Lord Jesus Christ. God's call in life includes family life, employment, social life, civic engagements and any other aspect of our everyday life.

God's call in life is secondary to the other 3 types of calls identified by Paul Helm. Unfortunately most Christians spend most of the time fulfilling their calling to responsibilities in the physical dimension.

The text in Ephesians 4:1-6 is specifically concerned about the concept of a call, but it is not just a call about the Christians relationship to the physical world. It is about a spiritual call; it is an eternal call to be in a favorable relationship with God forever.

Christians are instructed and exhorted to walk worthy of the calling with which they were called according to the Word of God. The interpretations of that one verse must equal the number of definitions given in Webster. The most popular interpretations are:

1) Secular employment - Totally unrelated to this text.

2) Unity - Call to unity - Just because a study Bible says walk in unity that is not inspired. I expect the popularization of the unity interpretation comes from the ecumenical movement. Organizational church unity is the goal of the ecumenical movement. Sacrifice all doctrine for unity.

A careful reading of this text will surely dismiss the idea that the call in this text is a call to be a good man on the job or a call to unity in the church. Paul was called; it happened to him. He did not call himself. The grammar and context is sufficient to dismiss the errors of interpreting this as a call to secular employment or a call to unity.

The "calling to which you were called" is an expanded reference to the call found in Ephesians 1:18, "that you may know the hope of God's call... ." This refers to God's effectual call. It refers to new life in Jesus Christ. It refers to the re-birth of the soul with new righteousness in Christ and eternal salvation.

Now in chapter 4 Paul makes a transition (therefore) urging the Gentiles and the Jews in the faith to live like they have been called by God to be God's child. Christians (the church) are called by God and with that calling comes a new way of living, which is summarized in this text.

The Christian is to walk or live with all humility and meekness. Humility is marked by a godly realization that one is totally dependent on God. A humble person doesn't gloat and take pride in the spotlight of life. There is no important feeling resulting from life's highway. Moses was humble, David was humble, Jesus Christ was humble, John Calvin was humble. (He requested no special funeral or grave marker at his death.) The long memorials among denominational leaders honoring the life of God's servants is not a sign of a healthy church. Not a mark of humility, it is a mark of pride. A memorial is something that a person leaves behind – the way he lived, the writings he left behind.

The Christian is to walk or live with longsuffering. Patience is the mark of a Christian who is willing to endure trouble in the face of opposition. Don't give up just because things get rough.

God's call is followed by a unique relationship not only with the Lord Jesus Christ, but with one another in the faith. God's call is evident when "bearing with one another in love" is prominent.

The Greek word from which we get the word *bearing* is actually two Greek words: *ana* (preposition - up) *exo* (verb - to hold) combined these two Greek words actually mean to *hold up*.

I think a better translation is "to encourage one another in love" therefore, "bear one another's sin burden" (Galatians 6:2). This is a unique relationship between Christians.

In the Christian life, Christians must be eager to keep the unity of the Spirit in the bond of peace. In this context the unity of the Spirit requires a unity of doctrine. Paul explains peace in terms of the middle wall of separation is broken down. The doctrine of Christ and the application of his saving grace is the same to Jew and Gentile. Christians understand saving grace because the Holy Spirit opens their eyes to understand the doctrine of grace, "For through Him we have access by one Spirit to the Father" (Ephesians 2:14-18).

The unity referred to is wrapped up into the 7 "ones."

> One body - the church - the church, which is His body.
> One Spirit - the Holy Spirit - not many spirits.
> One hope - The biblical use of the word hope is different than most contemporary usage, i.e. hope is optimism. Actually modern hope is what some people

would call wishful thinking. "I hope I win the sweepstakes." Biblical hope is a certain objective hope. Biblical hope is grounded in God's promises. For instance God calls his elect to trust Jesus Christ and his elect in turn hope (trust) in Christ for eternal life.

> One Lord
> One faith
> One baptism
> One God

The question every professing Christian should ask: "Does your calling glorify God?"

> Yes - If God has called you, there you will find glory.
> Yes - If God has called you, there you will find unity in your understanding of the nature and character of God and how you must relate to Him.

So then, are you living like a man, woman or child called by God? Does your life reflect a call by God or to put it another way, is the glory of God in your call? These are tough questions. As the Apostle Paul says I beseech you to walk worthy of the calling with which you were called.

13. The Grace of God for Ministry

Ephesians 4:7-16

The Christian life and calling is a gift from God, a gift of God's grace. God's grace does not depend on a person's station in life. The emphasis in this text is the gift of grace for ministry. Paul quotes from the Old Testament:

> When He ascended on high,
> He led captivity captive,
> And gave gifts to men.
> (New King James Version)

> When he ascended on high he led a host of captives and he gave gifts to men. (Revised Standard Version)

> When he ascended on high he led captives in his train and gave gifts to men. (New International Version)

This is an imprecatory prayer of David and speaking to God said: "You have ascended on high, you have led captivity captive; You have received gifts among men, Even from the rebellious...". (Psalm 68:18). Paul changed the Psalm in his letter to the Ephesians to refer to Christ, so that rather than receiving gifts, Christ gave gifts to men. Although much ink has been spilt over this verse there is no mystical allegory about this verse. It is a parenthesis and a preface to Paul's forth coming statement about God's call on the lives of His elect. What did Christ do for Christians to enjoy this great blessing?

What does it mean "He ascended" but that He also first descended into the lower parts of the earth. He who descended is also the One who ascended far above all the heavens, that He might fill all things.

This text teaches the humiliation and exaltation of Christ was necessary for Him to fulfill all righteousness so the church would receive the fullness of His blessing and a fore taste of His glory. The victory of Christ over sin and death gave Him full possession of His people. You might say his people follow his triumphant victory like captives in his train. The captives receive gifts from the victorious Christ. Their callings are not empty. Christ gives them what they need to fulfill their responsibilities.

Paul explains how Christ distributes some of these gifts. "And He Himself gave some to be apostles, some prophets, some evangelists, and some pastors and teachers..." (Ephesians 4:11). Just as God governs the invisible church, so God has given four particular offices to govern the visible church.

Apostles – This was a specific New Testament office that required an inspired messenger from God. The only ones that could fulfill this office had to witness Christ's resurrection or they were the recipients of special revelation, which was proven by the power of miracles.

Prophets – This office was given to those to speak forth the true doctrine of the Word of God. Agabus typifies this office (Acts 21:10). There were also many false prophets (Matthew 7:15).

Evangelists – This office indicates the spiritual gift of announcing the good news of God's saving grace. Philip is a notable example of an evangelist (Acts 21:8).

Pastor/Teacher – This is one office with two responsibilities.

One thing all these offices carry with them is the responsibility to preach and teach the whole counsel of God. Apostles and prophets in a proper sense have ended, but evangelists and pastor/teachers are necessary. A pastor is necessary to the edification of a congregation and I carry it one step further; a pastor is necessary for godly government in the church. Preaching is essential. The pastor/teacher has been called and Christ has given him the gift of preaching the whole counsel of God.

However, God never intended the gifted preacher to do all the work of God. In fact, the real preacher's gift is that of equipping or preparing every member in the church for ministry (service). The pastor gets the members ready to serve Christ, so the church will find strength and purpose in this wicked generation. The solemn task is to bring the church to maturity.

The level of maturity of the church is measured by width and depth. A mature church is not one that has a few people who grow up spiritually. The Word of God posits, "we all" have a responsibility to grow up spiritually (Ephesians 4:13). The depth of a mature church is measured by the unity of faith and the unity of the knowledge of the Son of God.

Faith and knowledge are absolutely necessary if one is to mature in the Christian religion. I find a serious lack of both in every branch of the church of our Lord. Faith means to believe in something or someone. Blind faith does not exist in reality. Knowledge refers to an acquaintance with biblical doctrine. Without faith and knowledge the church will not mature.

So we must ask the question: why are there so many immature churches. The question will find its answer in one or more of the following:

1. A lack of gifted pastors/teachers.
2. Gifted pastors/teachers are not doing their jobs.

3. The equipped saints fail to do their jobs.

There is a way to determine whether or not the church is mature. Paul uses four metaphors to describe an immature church:

1. The church acts like children.
2. They are tossed to and fro.
3. It is carried about with every wind of doctrine.
4. The church is influenced by the trickery of men into doctrinal error.

The mature church on the other hand speaks the truth in love. Even skilled theologians and Bible scholars sugar coat those 5 words: "speak the truth in love." One English Bible scholar said of this verse "love is the most important feature of Christianity." No! The most important feature of Christianity is Christ. It was the Lord Jesus Christ who spoke the truth in love in an ultimate sense. After feeding the 5000, many disciples turned away because Jesus spoke the truth in love. When Jesus was confronted by the religious leaders of His day, he spoke the truth in love.

Truth and love are inseparably connected. Throughout Scripture we find lovingkindness and truth face to face and back to back. Preaching the truth of God's wrath and the gospel of God's grace will bring maturity to the church.

Some Christians are more mature in Christ than others. Every Christian should ask these questions.

> Are you being fed a good diet of preaching?

> Are you receiving God's grace in the preaching and sacraments?

> Are you mature in the doctrine of Scripture?

Are you like-minded with the other members of the church?

Are you doing your share to cause the body of Christ to grow to maturity?

Only you can answer those questions. Those questions have nothing to do with personal preferences. They have to do with the law and the gospel. If you answered no to any of them, then the law has reminded you of your sin. If you answered them positively and have infallible assurance that your maturity in Christ is complete, because of His sacrifice for you, then the gospel has reminded you of God's glory in the ministry of the church.

14. The Grace of God's Truth

Ephesians 4:17-24

People do not die for ethics as an ethic. The ethical norms and moral practices of Christians express themselves because they believe, passionately believe something is right or wrong. They find occasions to act upon what they believe.

The question Christians have to ask is: why do they believe? Then they have to ask: How do they know or can they be assured they are right about what they believe? The inspired apostle Paul thought he was right even to the point of death.

1) Paul was a Christian ethicist.
2) Christian Ethics presuppose God's law.
3) Christian ethics are necessary for the church.

However, some Protestant theologians have robbed the church of a proper and biblical understanding of Christian ethics and morals. The "be good and do good" moralism that came out of the fundamentalist movement in this country settled in the laps of evangelical Christians.

It is unfortunate that professing evangelical believers tried to tackle the moral monster before his time. Many professing Christians believe that moral character is the reason we make decisions about what is right or wrong. The biblical doctrine teaches that morality is grounded in truth.

Jesus Christ was the Word and wherever you go with that you have to admit that the Word in John 1:1-14 was full of truth and truth is not irrational. A major theme in John is truth. The entire corpus of Scripture distills the truth attributed to God. God is rational, reasonable, and logical.

Truth is rational, reasonable, and logical. So is moral conduct. Christians cannot believe the truth of the gospel without understanding truth nor can they witness to the grace of God without some understanding of truth. The word truth is used 33 times in the book of Psalms. "Surely you desire truth in the inner parts; you teach me wisdom in the inmost place" (Psalm 51:6). Truth fills the depth of your being, your soul, your heart and life. "But as for me, my prayer is to Thee, O Lord, at an acceptable time; O God, in the greatness of Thy lovingkindness answer me with Thy saving truth" (Psalm 69:13). Truth reveals the saving power of God. "Teach me Thy way, O Lord; I will walk in Thy truth; Unite my heart to fear Thy name" (Psalm 86:11). Christians must not only believe truth, they must practice truth.

Truth transcends time, and cultures. The church of all ages is the pillar and foundation of truth. (See Romans 3:1,2; 2 Timothy 3:15.) The church in the Old Testament failed to hear God and truth left them. So you shall say to them, 'This is a nation that does not obey the voice of the LORD their God nor receive correction. Truth has perished and has been cut off from their mouth" (Jeremiah 7:28).

Biblical truth suggests an openness of the real and genuine rather than imaginary or spurious. Biblical truth is revealed to God's people, but to unbelievers, biblical truth is a mystery. You will never find the glory of God in a moral code until you first find the glory of God in His eternal truth.

The Word of God commands professing Christians to speak the "truth in love." Too often they want love to the exclusion of truth. I refer to the malady as psychological irrationalism. Rational inquiry is out and emotions do the talking.

It is much harder to dig for the truth than it is to ceaselessly muddle through words. To put it in street language some Christians talk until they think of something to say.

Ephesians

If you speak the truth in love, there is a release of truth in righteousness. Remember, you have been saved by grace through faith. The righteousness of Jesus Christ has called you to the work of ministry. God saved you:

    not because you are important
    not because of your money
    not because of your intellect
    not because of your charming countenance.
    You are saved for one purpose - to glorify God.

In the context of Ephesians chapter 4, you glorify God according to your call whether it's God's effective call in conversion, God's calling in life, or God's heavenly call.

Therefore, the Apostle Paul testifies that the church is different than all other people on this earth. "This I say, therefore, and testify in the Lord, that you should no longer walk as the rest of the Gentiles walk" (Ephesians 4:17).

How do unbelievers live? The Word of God states they live "in the futility of their mind." Futility is not the average household word. Some translate it vanity. The Greek word *mataiotes* essentially refers to emptiness, something useless.

The Greek word translated mind is *nous* and is used about 2 dozen times in the New Testament. I can't think of one place that the word mind does not refer to some aspect of rational capacity; the ability to think and reason.

Does it mean that the unbeliever cannot think and reason? Absolutely not, however unbelievers are more inclined to scholarship than to intellectual acumen.

What Paul does mean is that the unbeliever's life is frustrated. He can't find ultimate purpose. As the apostle Paul has already said unbelievers are "without Christ, being aliens from the commonwealth of Israel and strangers from the covenants of promise, having no hope and without God in the world" (Ephesians 2:12).

Why does Paul describe the mind of an unbeliever as an empty mind or a purposeless mind? The unbeliever has proximate purposes: recognition, honor, money, motives that have to do with this secular world. However, the unbeliever does not have ultimate purpose in the view of life.

Paul asserts that unbelievers walk in the futility of their minds because their understanding was darkened and they were alienated from the life of God. This is nothing more than a reference to the Fall of man and the doctrine of total depravity. Adam's rational abilities (reasoning or intellectual abilities) were not destroyed at the Fall, but his ability to think was confused and frustrated. Paul used similar language in his inspired letter to the Romans. "...[A]lthough they knew God, they did not glorify Him as God, nor were thankful, but became futile in their thoughts and their foolish hearts were darkened" (Romans 1:21).

Before Adam sinned, he was in perfect harmony with God, but after Adam's lapse he was alienated. Peace changed to war. Why were they alienated from God? It was "because of the blindness of their heart." It seems to me that Paul is simply employing the use of parallelism to make his point to believers at Ephesus and to all believers.

If you think that Christianity is a religion based on the believers moral uprightness, you don't understand Christianity. You've started at the wrong place. Christianity is based on the perfect work of Jesus Christ. Earlier in this letter Paul said "For we are His workmanship, created in Christ Jesus for good works, which God prepared beforehand that we should walk (live) in them" (Ephesians 2:10).

Christians should not give themselves over to lewdness, or to work all uncleanness with greediness. Isn't that morality? Isn't Paul concerned about Christian morals? I never said he wasn't. I said that Christianity doesn't begin with morality. Christianity begins with the renewing of your mind. The Word of God teaches: "put on the new man which was created according to God, in true righteousness and holiness" (Ephesians 4:24). This same doctrine is found in Paul's letter to the Colossians. There Paul refers to the "new man who is renewed in knowledge, according to the image of Him who created him" (Colossians 3:10)

> The renewing of the mind turns darkness into light.
> The renewing of the mind turns war into peace.

It is God who gives the light and God who gives the peace. Light and peace demands a new ethical norm.

As John Calvin said, "the proper purpose of the law finds its place among believers in whose hearts the Spirit of God already lives and reigns." The emphasis ought to be on "Already" because truth logically precedes morality.

You will never glorify God with your moral character until you know, understand, and embrace the truth as it is found in Christ Jesus; The truth of God and His sovereign nature and character; The truth about man and his dependence on God for all things in this life and the life to come.

15. The Grace of God's Commandments

Ephesians 4:25-32

Ephesians chapter 4 reflects a transition in the inspired Apostle's message to the church. Chapters 1 – 3 is primarily devoted to an explanation of our legal relationship with the triune God.

> In Him also we have obtained an inheritance being predestined according to the purpose of Him who works all things according to the counsel of His will, that we who first trusted in Christ should be to the praise of His glory" (Ephesians 1:11).

This phrase, "obtained an inheritance" is legal or forensic language.

Theologians use the Latin phrase *justitia alienum* meaning an "alien righteousness." Christ *declares* one righteous. Christ does not *make* one righteous. This legal language speaks to Christians about their legal relationship with the triune God. Triune refers to the Trinity.

Therefore, we must not leave out the 3rd person of the Trinity.

> In Him you also trusted after you heard the word of truth, the gospel of your salvation; in whom also, having believed, you were sealed with the Holy Spirit of promise. (Ephesians 1:13)

This focus on our relationship with the triune God is prevalent throughout Ephesians chapters 1 -3 and precedes Christian morality.

The shift from predominately legal language to moral language is found in the first verse of Chapter 4 with the use of the word "therefore." The inspired Apostle warns Christians to walk worthy of the calling with which they were called. Christians have been called to a right and peaceful relationship with God through the Lord Jesus Christ.

A right relationship will show itself with right living. Christians are also called to live according to a Christian ethic. Now the language has shifted to moral language. I use the word shift because there is a transition. The result of new life in Christ is that Christians no longer have an empty head for spiritual things. They have been enlightened so that the mind comprehends the truth of the law and the gospel. They are no longer alienated from God. The Christian must put on the new man, which was created according to God, in true righteousness and holiness.

Something follows God's call on the Christian. It is a new way of life. The new way of life is often referred to as Christian morality. Christian morals are expressed by a lengthy set of imperatives found in the Bible. An imperative is a command to do something or do not do something. There are hundreds of imperatives in Scripture.

I only found a couple of imperatives until this present reading in the book of Ephesians and they were not associated with Christian morality. In Ephesians 4:25-32 there are 11 imperatives. A cursory reading of this text might lead one to believe that Paul has the 10 commandments in mind. Although Paul refers to a couple of the 10 commandments specifically, this is not a lesson on the 10 commandments. There does not appear to be any logical order to these imperatives and there is no order grammatically.

Some of them are imperatives of command so that it is a positive command. Some of them are imperatives of prohibition. This is the kind of command issued with the purpose of stopping an action already in progress.

Ephesians

Like anyone else converted to Christianity, particularly a conversion later in life, the Ephesians brought immoral garbage with them into their Christian experience.

We shouldn't be shocked today when we find all sorts of pagan activity in the church. We've allowed it. It's the fault of the teaching and ruling elders. If unconverted people are admitted into membership of the church, those unconverted members will turn into unconverted elders.

The inspired Apostle Paul had identified church members acting like pagans, so he lays out a set of commands according to the moral law of God to warn these professing Christians of their immorality.

I want to lay out these commands in some logical order rather than the chronological order in which they are recorded in Scripture.

There is a close relationship between those positive commands that instruct Christians to do something and the commands of prohibition that instruct Christians to stop doing something.

There are five positive commands in this text:

verse 25 - speak truth
verse 26 - be angry
verse 28 - work hard - 1 Tim. 5:17
verse 31 - Let all bitterness, anger, wrath, clamor, and blasphemy be removed
verse 32 - Be kind to one another

There are six negative commands:

verse 26 - Do not sin
verse 26 - Do not let the sun go down on your anger
verse 27 - Do not give the Devil an opportunity
verse 28 - Let him who steals steal no longer

verse 29 - Let no corrupt word proceed from your mouth
verse 30 - Do not grieve the Holy Spirit

The first positive command is speak truth. Why did Paul begin his moral lesson with truth. I believe there are many reasons, but I will only mention a couple.

1st - Truth is the starting point for all intelligent discourse, so truth requires the right use of words.
2nd - Truth is a self-evident axiom.

Christians cannot witness of God's grace unless they understand truth and therefore cannot really be a part of the church. The Bible teaches the church is the pillar and foundation of truth and I might add the truth which transcends time and cultures. The Psalmist put it in these terms: "For His lovingkindness is great toward us, and the truth of the Lord is everlasting" (Psalm 117:2). The Psalm teaches that truth is not relative, never has and never will be. Now consider how truth relates to 3 of Paul's do not commands.

verse 27 - If we speak the truth, then we will not give the devil an opportunity for deceit for which he is the expert.

verse 29 - If we speak the truth, then no corrupt word will proceed from our mouth.

verse 30 - If we speak the truth, then we will not grieve the Holy Spirit.

Righteous anger is the mark of a Christian, but righteous anger must not turn into sin. When the mind has been renewed Christians are commanded to be angry but not a selfish, undisciplined, uncontrolled and sinful anger. The Lord Jesus Christ became angry; He looked at the Pharisees with anger (Mark 3:5). Jesus made a whip and drove the money changers out of the Temple (John 2:13-15).

Paul's do not commands in Ephesians are associated with the command to be angry. "Do not let the sun go down on your anger..." (Ephesians 4:26). Does that mean each day at sundown Christians should be happy with the murdering abortionists, the evil and corruption in the world and even in the church. The positive command in verse 31 is given to clarify and confirm the negative command in verse 26. The command in verse 31 is passive. The command is simply "Let it be removed!" Remove what? All bitterness, anger, wrath, clamor, and blasphemy. These things are removed by the power of the Spirit working in you.

The next positive command is, "Let him who stole steal no longer, but rather let him labor, working with his hands what is good, that he may have something to give him who has need" (Ephesians 4:28). It simply states a biblical principle commonly known as work hard. If you work hard, you will not have to steal.

The last positive command is "be kind to one another" (Ephesians 4:32) which summarizes the 2nd table of the 10 commandments.

God calls the church to new life in Christ and along with new life comes a new walk or a new way of life. This new life is marked by:

    Truthful speech
    Righteous anger
    Hard work
    Remove bitterness
    Stop outrageous behavior
    Blathering confusion and blasphemy
    Showing kindness to one another.

Martin Murphy

It's the law, gospel, law. The law convicts one of sin, the gospel saves one from sin, and then the law becomes the standard by which the Christian lives.

16. The Grace of God's Forgiveness

Ephesians 4:32

The only way to know how to forgive one another is to model our forgiveness after God's forgiveness. The Word of God tells the Christian to "be kind to one another, tenderhearted, forgiving one another, even as God in Christ forgave you" (Ephesians 4:32). Notice the manner in which God forgives. "I will forgive their iniquity, and their sin I will remember no more" (Jeremiah 31:34). This text does not mean that God is forgetful, but after God forgives, He does not bring up the sin again. God is omniscient. He cannot forget anything, but He simply does not bring the imputed sin of Adam or the actual sins into account after He forgives. "As far as the east is from the west, so far has He removed our transgressions from us" (Psalm. 103:12). How a Christian feels about sin and forgiveness does not determine the reality of forgiveness. What counts is objective reality, which is found in the Word of God. Christians must judge according to truth, not how they feel about truth. God doesn't forgive because He feels like it. God forgives because of His grace and mercy.

Does anyone deserve forgiveness? The Bible answers the question with a rhetorical question that every person ought to ask. "If You, Lord, should mark iniquities, O Lord, who could stand?" (Psalm. 130:3). God, by His pure grace, forgives you of your multiplied sins against Him. When Christians say "we believe in the forgiveness of sins" they believe they have been forgiven of the thousands upon thousands of sins that have been removed by the sacrifice of the Lord Jesus Christ. Then likewise, by grace, Christians forgive each other. In His model prayer Jesus instructs His people to call upon God and ask for forgiveness of sins (Luke 11:1-4). I have never personally heard of a Christian refusing to ask God for forgiveness of sins. However, it is a common habit for Christians to refuse to ask one another for forgiveness. In the Lord's model prayer Christians are instructed to ask God to forgive their sins and to forgive everyone who is indebted to them. The purpose, mission, and ministry of the church will be stigmatized because Christians who have offended and sinned against other Christians have not asked for forgiveness, which means a debt remains unpaid. The word "debt" is important. The Lord's model prayer refers to a debtor. This portion of the prayer means that when one Christian sins against another Christian, the offending party has an obligation to the offended party or to put it another way, that person has a debt to pay. This debt does not refer to a financial transaction between Christians. It does not mean that God's forgiveness may be earned by forgiving a brother or sister in Christ. If Christians practice or refuse to practice the biblical doctrine of forgiveness, it is evidence of a spiritual condition.

When the Bible commands Christians to "forgive one another" the necessity and emphasis is on mutual forgiveness. The doctrine is very clear. God, by His pure grace, forgives the sinner of his or her multiplied sins against God, and then the forgiven sinner must forgive others who sin against him or her. When Christians forgive, truly forgive, they are simply following the example of the Lord and give evidence of the grace of the Lord Jesus Christ present in the soul. If you are not able to forgive others who have offended you and sinned against you, then you have not received any forgiveness from God. This is hard doctrine for many professing Christians to accept, but the Word of God is very clear. Listen to the words that come directly from the mouth of the Lord Jesus Christ. "For if you forgive men their trespasses, your heavenly Father will also forgive you. But if you do not forgive men their trespasses, neither will your Father forgive your trespasses"

(Matthew 6:14, 15). First the Lord addresses it positively: "For if you forgive men their trespasses, your heavenly Father will also forgive you." Then the Lord addresses it negatively: "But if you do not forgive men their trespasses, neither will your Father forgive your trespasses." This does not mean that God's forgiveness is contingent upon you forgiving another person. It does mean that you will be compelled to forgive the other person if God has forgiven you. To forgive the other person means to remove from your mind any wrath, hatred, or desire for revenge. To forgive means to willingly, gladly, generously, and finally forget any injustice you may have experienced in your relationship with the other person. The Word of God is so clear and so loud I do not understand how Christians can misread it or misinterpret it, or misunderstand it. Christians must forgive the way God forgives. Forgiveness must come from the heart. Forgiveness comes from the depth of the soul involving the mind, will, and emotions.

Jesus told the parable of the unforgiving servant. It is the story of one person that was forgiven a large debt, but that same man refused to forgive someone else a much smaller debt (Matthew 18:21-35). The conclusion to the parable should be thought provoking. "So My heavenly Father also will do to you if each of you, from his heart, does not forgive his brother his trespasses" (Matthew 18:35). The warnings in Scripture should cause every believer to search the heart to know what to do.

> These are the things you shall do: Speak each man the truth to his neighbor; Give judgment in your gates for truth, justice, and peace; Let none of you think evil in your heart against your neighbor; And do not love a false oath. For all these are things that I hate says the Lord. (Zechariah 8:16, 17)

There are other factors that are relative to the biblical doctrine of forgiveness. Like any other teaching in Scripture, the whole counsel of God must come under scrutiny. For instance confession, repentance, and reconciliation are all connected with forgiveness.

> God commands confession for forgiveness. Confess means you acknowledge the sin and agree with your brother that it is sin. (1 John 1:9; James 5:16; Matthew 18:15)
>
> Repentance is necessary if the confession is sincere and true; Take heed to yourselves. If your brother sins against you, rebuke him; and if he repents, forgive him. (Luke 17:3)
>
> Reconciliation is just as important as repentance. Forgiveness means that the sin will never be brought up again and the relationship is restored. (Matthew 5:24; 2 Corinthians 5:18-19; Psalm 103:12)

Too often Christians dismiss the doctrine of reconciliation. I have heard professing Christians say, "I'll forgive, but I will not be reconciled." The Bible makes it clear that reconciliation is an essential part of forgiveness. To deny the doctrine of reconciliation would be like God saying, "I'll forgive you, but I do not want to ever see you again." The Bible speaks of reconciliation before the judgment day (Matthew 5:21-26). This text is for the occasion when you remember that your Christian brother believes you have sinned against him. It is one of the most difficult sayings of the Lord Jesus Christ: "You will by no means get out of there" (Matthew 5:26). This certainly implies that two Christian believers are in a broken relationship because of sin. Everything possible should be done to resolve the broken relationship so the two parties may be reconciled. If one person refuses to forgive, then the guilt will rest upon the person who refused to forgive. This is so important and may sound strange, but study the Word of God carefully. God promises to forgive, but woe to the person who refuses to forgive and be reconciled.

Reconciliation means peace. Do you want peace with God and peace with other Christians? If the answer is yes, I urge you to remember the words of the Psalmist. "I acknowledged my sin to Thee, And my iniquity I did not hide; I said, 'I will confess my transgressions to the Lord'; And Thou didst forgive the guilt of my sin" (Psalm 32:5).

The one word I want and I hope you want written on your headstone is: Forgiven.

17. The Grace of God in His Wrath

Ephesians 5:1-7

The command is "be imitators of God."

Unfortunately, some professing Christian preachers and teachers do not understand the system of doctrine taught in Scripture. These men use this text to deify human nature. They take the word imitators to mean that Christians have a *theanthropic* nature. The term *theanthropic* derives from the Greek words *theos* translated God and *anthropos* translated man combined into one word *theanthrophic* which refers to divine and human in one nature. A heresy wherein the human and divine natures of Jesus Christ were combined. The *theanthropic* nature is often seen as a humanized divine nature or a deified human nature.

The word imitator is translated from a Greek word, which essentially means to mimic. In his letter to the Thessalonian Church the inspired Apostle wrote, "you became followers of us and of the Lord." They imitated the apostle who imitated the Lord. The profound, yet simple language for a dear child of God is to mimic or follow the ways of the Lord Jesus Christ.

The Ephesian Church and by extension Christians in every generation are commanded to "walk in love." These 2 commandments (imitate and walk in love) are collateral to each other. The question to ponder is: how is it possible to "walk in love, as Christ also has loved us... ." Christ's love for the church is best expressed by John Calvin's famous words *finitum non capax infinitum*. Those Latin words translate to the English in this manner: "the finite cannot comprehend the infinite." Man cannot fully understand God and neither is man able to love to the same degree that Christ loved the church. Nevertheless, Christians are commanded to live a life that reflects the character of godly love.

There is no justice or truth, if Christians distort God's love, which is so easy to do since Christians are sinful creatures. They have a tendency to turn biblical love into a passionate cultural love or an erotic sensual love of the worldly nature. The biblical love described in this text refers to God's love for his church, a love that is intense, deeply personal, unique, spontaneous, sovereign, eternal, and infinite.

If God's love is sovereign and eternal, then God demonstrates His love in all His attributes and characteristics. The activity of God's love is comprehensive because it touches every aspect of His kingdom especially God's justice, which is so manifest in Isaiah 61:8. There the Lord God omnipotent speaking through the prophet Isaiah says: "For I, The Lord, love justice."

Dr. John Gerstner in a sermon said, "God's justice is manifested in mercy (love), but especially in wrath." One of God's characteristics is His wrath. Although it may sound strange to say "a loving God is a wrathful God," it is not strange to the Word of God. We come to this text and discover God is glorified in His wrath.

Yes, God is glorified even when his anger is provoked by the immoral acts of individuals. The Bible teaches the wrath of God comes upon the sons of disobedience, not only in the Ephesian text, but also in the Old Testament.

> Therefore thus says the Lord God: Behold, My anger and MY fury will be poured out on this place - on man and on beast, on the trees of the field and on the fruit of the ground. And it will burn and not be quenched. (Jeremiah 7:20)

That God's wrath is being be poured out on the human race is unquestionable. The activity of the wrath of God coming upon the sons of disobedience is an ongoing present activity. To put it in simple terms, God is angry at this present time and demonstrates his wrath at the present time. It is necessary to review Paul's earlier instruction.

> And you He made alive, who were dead in trespasses and sins, in which you once walked according to the course of this world, according to the prince of the power of the air, the spirit who now works in the sons of disobedience, among whom also we all once conducted ourselves in the lusts of our flesh, fulfilling the desires of the flesh and of the mind, and were by nature children of wrath, just as the others. (Ephesians 2:1-3)

The wrath of the Lord comes upon people for any number of different reasons. The Bible explains in terms of how "they mocked (the Israelites, the Old Testament church) the messengers of God, despised His words, and scoffed at His prophets, until the wrath of the Lord arose against His people. . ." (2 Chronicles 36:16). God's wrath was against professing believers. In the gospel of John we see the wrath of God particularly abiding upon unbelievers.

We've now come to a very delicate, very complicated, but very evident fact that our text expresses in no uncertain terms.

1) - Unbelievers will not inherit the kingdom of God.

2) - Believers are not to participate in the evil and wicked ways of unbelievers.

What are those evil wicked ways? The Apostle Paul says they are as follows:

> fornicators,
> unclean people,
> covetous men,
> idolaters.

There is an expanded version of these sins in Galatians 5:19 and 1 Corinthians 6:9,10 and especially in Romans 1:28-32. The most prominent is idolatry. Idolatry is probably a reference to the 1st and 2nd commandments of the 10 commandments given to Moses. The 1st commandment tells us to worship God and God alone.

1) Acknowledge and adore God
2) Fear God and at the same time trust God
3) We have to love God and obey God

An idolater is one who at any point and time doesn't do these things and on the contrary, puts his or her trust in anything else.

> If we trust our riches, then riches becomes our god.
> If we trust in any worldly thing, it becomes our god.
> If we trust our wisdom, it becomes our god.
> If we trust in our own ability, it becomes our god.
> If we trust our civility, it becomes our god.
> If we love or give attention to anything other than the true and living God, we have violated this 1st commandment.

The world demonstrates a pantheon of deities: career, possessions, greed, self-esteem, family, friends, entertainment, fashion, gluttony and a host of philosophical and theological views. Idolatry may be measured by degrees and the Bible declares, "For whoever shall keep the whole law and yet stumble in one point, he is guilty of all" (James 2:10). The inspired Apostle Paul described his personal experience. "For what I am doing, I do not understand. For what I will to do, that I do not practice; but what I hate, that I do" (Romans 7:15).

Does the Apostle then tell us that we have a license to sin? Absolutely not! Then how do we reconcile these two seemingly contrary views? The wrath of God has been poured out on the whole human race. The unbeliever will eternally reap the fury of God's wrath.

The Christian believer will experience the wrath of God for particular sins, but will be eternally redeemed from his or her sin and sins by the finished work of Jesus Christ and His righteousness credited to their account. One quote from Jonathan Edwards may be helpful as well: "nothing preserves you one moment from suffering this wrath but the mere pleasure of the angry God."

The difference between the believer and the unbeliever is that the believer endeavors to keep the law of God to glorify God. It is his or her goal in life. But when he or she comes short, they rush to the cross of Christ. The believer has a deep seated desire to reverence God with perfect obedience. Christians must be willing to say afflict me Lord, as thou will in this life, so I may escape the wrath to come. God will be glorified in His wrath!

18. The Grace of God in the Children of Light

Ephesians 5:7-14

Paul warns Christians not to participate with the sons of disobedience in evil things. Satan works in the sons of disobedience. Paul reminded the Ephesians of the condition of their soul before Christ.

Paul's comparison of darkness and light is properly an antithesis. Or to put it another way, the inspired apostle puts all humans beings into one category or the other. Those two antithetical categories are described as dark and light. The Word of God describes Christians in terms of "were once darkness." Notice the language. Christians were not once in darkness, but rather they were darkness.

Paul uses this word darkness about a dozen times in his inspired writing. He also refers to people being "in darkness" such as Romans 2:20 where he commends the Roman Christians for being a light to those who are in darkness. These two metaphors dark and light richly adorn the Word of God. The Lord Jesus said, "I have come as a light into the world that whoever believes in Me should not abide in darkness" (John 12:46).

Sometimes we can best describe what something is not better than we can describe what a thing is. If we say the car is not moving, then we mean it is stationary. The same analogy may be used to describe darkness and light.

This portion of God's word reminds Christians of what they were for some specific period of time, but now they are something else. Christians were formally dark, but now they are light.

Paul's metaphor "you were once darkness" is not a reference to the environment, but a reference to their state of being. It is a major topic in the Bible and Paul refers to it often.

>Ephesians 2:1 - You were dead in trespasses and sin.

>Ephesians 2:2 - You once walked according to the course of this world.

>Ephesians 2:3 - You were by nature a child of wrath.

>Ephesians 2:12 - You were strangers to the covenant of promise, having no hope and without God.

>Ephesians 4:17 - In times past, you had a vain mind, your understanding was darkened, and you were alienated from the life of God.

Darkness is a symbol of Satan and his angels, a symbol associated with words like sin, disobedience, rebellion, ignorance, blindness, falsehood, hatred, wrath, shame, strife, and bondage. Those words sound like gloom and doom, but I have good news for Christians; the epoch of this darkness has ended for Christians who are now light in the Lord.

These metaphors "darkness and light" are often used in Scripture. None is more prominent than the reference Jesus used in the Sermon on the Mount. "You are the light of the world" (Matthew 5:14).

The word light has a rich heritage in the Old Testament.

>Psalm 27:1 - The Lord is my light.

> Psalm 37:6 - He will make your righteousness shine as the light.
>
> Isaiah 42:6 - I will keep you and will make you to be a covenant for the people and a light for the Gentiles.
>
> Proverbs 6:23 - For these commands are a lamp, this teaching is a light.

The New Testament reveals the theological importance of light.

> John 8:12 - Jesus said, "I am the light of the world."
>
> Jesus identifies Himself to the church as the light, but is the visible church commending the light of Christ to the world?
>
> 1 John 1:5 - This is the message we have heard from him and declare to you: God is light.

Ancient people understood darkness. Light was precious and important and thus not to be hid. Do you hide the light of your soul from the unconverted person who desires to persecute you? The condition of natural man is spiritual darkness, but Christians are the light. You might want to ask yourself the question: How am I light?

The Bible has the answer. "Walk as children of light (for the fruit of the Spirit is in all goodness, righteousness, and truth), finding out what is acceptable to the Lord" (Ephesians 5:8-10).

I know of no sensible way to interpret this metaphorical language except that children of light (Christians) ought to show evidence of the presence of the Light in them so that the light in them will shine in a dark world. The evidence of that Light is found in all goodness, righteousness, and truth.

The evidence of the light is in all goodness. When we use the word good, it reflects the quality of the thing to which it refers. Christians ought to seek the good in every dimension of life. The evidence of the light is in all righteousness "And having been set free from sin, you became slaves of righteousness" (Romans 6:18). The evidence of light is in all truth.

Truth is indispensable and inseparably connected with goodness and righteousness. Where goodness may emphasize the affections, especially in its relation to the aesthetic dimension of our being and righteousness as evidence of the light focuses on our moral condition, truth is necessary to the Christian mind.

The absence of an understanding of truth or a disregard for truth may mean an absence of light. Truth seems to be a consistent topic in Paul's letter to the Ephesians.

> Ephesians 1:11 - In Him you also trusted, after you heard the word of truth.
>
> Ephesians 4:11 - speak the truth in love.
>
> Ephesians 4:21 - the truth is in Jesus.

How can we know the truth? There are philosophical and theological implications. The simple formula for Christians; The Bible is the truth.

The will of God is found in the Word of God. In the Word of God you will find what is acceptable to the Lord in worship and life. It was Martin Luther who taught the Bible has 2 parts and everything in the Bible comes under one or the other - the law and the gospel.

Ephesians

God's Law should bring discomfort, but not despair. The gospel should bring comfort, but not arrogance. Where there is no truth, there is no light. If there is light, there cannot be darkness. "Therefore He says: Awake, you who sleep, Arise from the dead, and Christ will give you light" (Ephesians 5:14).

The Lord God omnipotent calls His people out of darkness into light so that as the inspired prophet Isaiah says: "the glory of the Lord is risen upon you." May the children of light glorify the Lord who gave them that Light.

19. The Grace of God in Wise Living

Ephesians 5:15- 21

The Bible never teaches dry cold stuffy doctrine, as many in this day and age seem to think. Neither does the Bible teach just practical tips for good living. The Bible does teach a true doctrine that is always practical and useful for Christian living.

The doctrine of God's eternal decrees is often thought of as a complicated and dehumanizing philosophy. On the contrary God's eternal decrees have very practical applications. Just think about it. God is independent, eternal, unchangeable, and He is not derived from anything. Humans on the other hand are dependent, temporal, and mutable and they derive their very substance from an independent Being.

If that independent eternal Being is the triune God, and He decides to give me, you, or anyone else a place in His eternal kingdom, that seems very practical to me. I deserve nothing, yet He gives me everything. That is very practical indeed.

Christians have often associated the practical things of the world with wisdom. The inspired Apostle Paul refers to the wisdom of this world in a pejorative sense when the Corinthian Church depended on worldly wisdom. The apostle does not deny worldly wisdom in every sense of the word.

Wisdom is a word that describes the quality or condition of a person. A wise person is thought of as one who has discernment and understanding, one who can give good advice. A wise person may possess those characteristics, but the Bible speaks of wisdom in a deeper more significant way.

In chapter one of Ephesians Paul refers to the spirit of wisdom and revelation. Paul prayed that the church may have a spirit of wisdom and revelation. There is human wisdom of which Paul speaks in his letter to the Corinthian Church and the Roman Church. In the Ephesian letter wisdom takes on a different meaning. The Ephesian Christians were told to be wise.

The English word wise derives from the Greek word *sophia*. The word unwise or foolish in our text is *asophia* in verse 15, but he uses the Greek word for foolish in verse 17. Even though the word unwise is used in verse 15, Scripture reveals that fools despise wisdom (Proverbs 1:7). In another place the Bible refers to "Wisdom is in the sight of him who has understanding, but the eyes of a fool are on the ends of the earth" (Proverbs 17:24).

There is another commandment that deserves particular attention.

> See then that you walk circumspectly (Ephesians 5:15, NKJV).
>
> Be careful how you walk (Ephesians 5:15, NAS).
>
> See ye carefully how you walk (My translation from the Greek text).

The command is see; the resulting action is walk (live). The emphasis is on the attention you give to the way you live. To put it in a question: how do Christians know how to live?

Serious Bible study is more often than not despised in the church today. The Bible makes it clear that Christian education is the sole responsibility of the church, yet very little of it takes place in the church. I fear that the largest part of Sunday School teachers in evangelical churches teach heresy to a greater or lesser degree on a regular basis. I also fear that most of them are not qualified, either with authority or gifts to teach the Word of God, according to biblical standards. In spite of the church's error, it is still the responsibility of the church to teach its members how to live wisely.

The Word of God does teach that an unwise or a foolish person does not know how to live wisely. It is necessary to understand the will of the Lord to live wisely and the only way a person can understand the will of the Lord is to know the Word of God.

A flimsy, pietistic, cursory, understanding of the Word of God is a shame and disgrace for any professing Christian. Even those who do study the Bible often have no concern for consistency and coherency. For a Christian to live wisely, the Christian must carefully study the Word of God, so the Christian will accurately understand the will of God. Wisdom is associated with discernment and stewardship.

Careful accurate instruction is necessary because the days are evil. It could be interpreted "age of evil" beginning with the fall of Adam. Christians are in a state of *symbiosis*. The word *symbiosis* is used in biology to refer to "the living together in intimate association or even close union with two dissimilar organisms."

The Christian has been redeemed and adopted into the family of God. His understanding has been enlightened. If properly equipped he is ready for the work of ministry. Unfortunately, at the same time some professing Christians cling to the evil in this evil age. Why would professing Christians cling to darkness? I don't know, but I do know that the Bible teaches Christians are light in a dark world.

Christian *symbiosis* has the Christian who is the light, living together in the same union with darkness. Unfortunately many professing Christians seem to believe that they can live like that, but they are deceived.

This evil age is a playground for Satan to deceive people.

>There is gross moral deceit.
>There is gross intellectual deceit.

There is gross relativistic deceit.
There is gross pragmatic and utilitarian deceit.
There is gross theological deceit.

There is corruption on every side:

> corrupt theology
> corrupt church government
> corrupt civil government
> corrupt familial order
> corrupt educational institutions
> corrupt social organizations
> The corruption is endless in this evil age in which we live.

The corruption, fraud, and deceit have and always will exist until the Lord returns for His church. Christians should disenfranchise themselves from the evils of this age and live carefully and accurately according to the Word of God. Paul commanded the Ephesian Church to "redeem the time." Make the most of the time God has given you. I hate it when people tell me the church cannot be reformed. That is contrary to the Word of God. The phrase in verse 16 "redeeming the time" literally means "buy up the time." Redeeming the time has nothing to do with gaining time or losing time. You can't create one extra moment for your life and Satan cannot steal one moment from your life. God has ordained how many minutes we have to serve Him and nothing can change His ordination. Redeeming the time has to do with making the best use of every circumstance as God providentially brings it your way. Maximize your gifts!

If Christians live according to their profession, they should seek to be free of the evil that plagues the church at this time. The remedy is simple, "do not be drunk with wine but be filled with the Spirit." Paul uses a common vice, drunkenness, to illustrate how a Christian should not live. Drunkenness is a sin, but the immorality of drunkenness is not the primary interest here. Drunkenness is a metaphor for disorder and confusion. Drunkenness dehumanizes a rational intelligent creature with its accompanying depressive effects. Who wants to live like that? Certainly not a wise Christian.

A wise Christian wants to live wisely, carefully, and accurately according to the Word of God. Such a way of living is found among those who are filled with the Spirit of God. There is a sense of joy and thanksgiving.

The Holy Spirit empowers the Christian to live a harmonious, content and satisfying life. The Spirit filled soul hates living in a drunken stupor and much prefers a sharp mind that is intellectually keen. The Spirit filled soul is inclined to good and truth rather than evil and deceit. The Spirit filled soul expresses the joy of Christian love in mutual submission to other Christians.

Pray that the Holy Spirit of God will empower you to live wisely and prepare yourself to live wisely according to the Word of God. The church will find the glory of God in wise living.

20. The Grace of God in a Godly Marriage

Ephesians 5:22-33

Paul wrote this inspired letter to Christians. The early chapters of Ephesians contain alleged difficult doctrines such as predestination. Some theologians tend to think the moral imperatives in the latter chapters are not God centered.

Nothing could be further from the truth. Every aspect of Christianity (true Christianity) is God centered. God created the soul and body and the Bible teaches the church that God governs the soul and body of all people, but the Christian soul and body in a special way. Many professing Christians think salvation and Hell insurance is the primary reasons for believing the doctrines of the Christian religion. That is simply not so. The Doctrine of the Christian religion instructs the child of God in every aspect of life.

This text of Scripture instructs the church relative to the most intimate of all human relationships, the marital relationship. The inspired apostle uses the analogy of the relationship of Christ to the church to explain the glorious nature of marriage. I say glorious marriage because marriage began with God's grace and will end with God's grace.

The Old Testament reference found in verse 31 is profound beyond human understanding. "For this reason a man shall leave his father and mother and be joined to his wife, and the two shall become one flesh" (Genesis 2:24).

This is one of 3 creational ordinances given to our pre-fall father, Adam. These are universal ordinances given for the benefit of the human race and God's glory. The marriage ordinance is unique in the sphere of human relationships;

"leave cleave and become one flesh." Why is the marriage ordinance in a state of upheaval? Why is the institution of marriage in such a state of disrepair? It seems the glory of God has left the marriage. The reason the glory of God has left the marriage is because the regulative principle has left the Christian arena.

Christianity has something to say about every aspect and dimension of our existence. To put it in different terms, Christians are governed by the Word of God. Christians must submit to the Word of God because it is the regulative principle that regulates marriage. God's plan for creation begins with order and harmony, "submitting to one another in the fear of God" (Ephesians 5:21).

The Greek word translated submit literally refers to order or to be subject to place or arrange one thing under another. As a military term to submit to someone was used to mean coming under the authority of a superior. To whom do Christians submit?

> 1) Submit to the triune God. Submit to God and resist the devil. (Ephesians 5:24; Hebrews 12:9; James 4:7)
>
> 3) Submit to the elders of the church. (1 Peter 5)
>
> 4) Submit to the management and role order that God has assigned within the family unit. (Titus 2:5; Ephesians 5:22)
>
> 5) Submit to the Government authorities. (Titus 3:1)
>
> 6) Submit to the economic station in life where God has placed you. (Titus 2:9)

Submission within the family and more specifically the command, "Wives submit to your own husbands, as to the

Ephesians

Lord" (Ephesians 5:22). Blind and blanket submission is never mentioned in the Bible. However, no submission leads to anarchy and absolute submission leads to tyranny.

Although anarchy and tyranny are present, to a greater or lesser degree in many marriages, the concept of submission usually falls under one of three categories.

Patriarchy
Matriarchy
Democracy

Godly submission from a biblical perspective is difficult because of the sin nature. Five enemies to godly submission are:

>1) Self-centeredness - A person who is governed by the thought that everything revolves around him or her.
>
>2) Dictatorial - Another aspect of the self by lording it over others. I call it having private agendas.
>
>3) Individualistic - I want to be myself. My opinions are the ones that count and if I can't have it my way I will not play in the game.
>
>4) Thoughtlessness - One who is unconcerned with respect to the position, needs, desires and welfare of others.
>
>5) Self-seeking - One who is interested in the outcome only for the benefit of self.

The greatest enemy to submission and the most destructive is disorder. The best antidote for disorder is order and that is what Paul means when he says we should be filled with the Spirit. God's Spirit cannot produce disorder; only harmony.

The Spirit of God enlightens the mind with respect to truth. Therefore, it is important to grasp the concept of truth relating to order and disorder. Think of it this way: If there is disorder, then no one is in charge (anarchy). If there is order then someone has been given authority to maintain order (theocracy).

The Bible teaches the husband is the head of the wife, as also Christ is the head of the church. It is an eternal concept of headship and submission prescribed by an orderly eternal estate.

The concept of submission is not complicated. Look at the end of verse 24. The wife is to submit to their own husbands in everything. However, the biblical concept of submission is difficult to practice.

Dr. Robert L. Dabney put it in these terms and I shall quote so as not to add or take away from these most profound words. Dr. Dabney said,

The wife must obey the husband in the sense of conceding to him the final decision of joint domestic questions, within the bound of her higher duty to God and conscience or the husband must obey the wife, or the marriage is virtually annulled. (Practical Philosophy, p. 367)

There are 2 non-negotiable propositions in his exposition.

1) Obey the husband within the bounds of her higher duty to God and conscience. (Obey God rather than man.)

2) If she does not obey her husband (unless he has told her to think or act in a way that is unbiblical) the marriage is virtually annulled.

If a husband submits to his wife, he has sinned and if there is no submission there is no marriage. One word will sum up the role of the wife in marriage: submit.

Likewise, one word will sum up the role of the husband in marriage: love. The Christian marriage does not exist if the husband does not love his wife just as Christ loved the church and gave Himself for her. Husbands are you willing to give your life for your wife? Are you willing to sacrifice everything for your bride? Christ did. It is the duty of the husband to love his wife so he may be the instrument for the sanctification of his wife.

The word love, as it is used in this letter, has no reference to sensual and friendly love that is propagated in the English speaking western world. The love in our text is a distinctive kind of love. It is Christian love. It is the kind of love that is sacrificial whether it is a love in confrontation or a love in encouragement, it is a godly love.

Looking back over the past 60 years I conclude the church is in a state of disorder and lacks a proper understanding of God's prescribed order for submission and love in the marriage.

I do not have a 3 or 5 step answer for this disorder. I do have a one step answer: Submit yourself to the Word of God and pray for the Spirit of God to enlighten your mind, to incline your will and motivate your emotions so you will find the glory of God in a godly marriage.

21. The Grace of God in Order and Authority

Ephesians 6:1-9

There is a fundamental general principle in Scripture that will help Christians walk worthy and walk with wisdom. "Submit to one another in the fear of God" (Ephesians 5:21). Submission is necessary in God's form of government if the church expects order and authority to prevail. Order and authority is an expression of God's nature and character. The church cannot separate submission, order, and authority. They all fit together. This text has another command for the church.

The command is "to obey." The general principle given in the command to obey is that authority demands respect. In God's government certain people have authority over others such as the Army officer in Matthew chapter 8. He wanted Jesus to heal his servant and he understood that Jesus had the authority to heal and stated it by analogy. He told Jesus:

> For I also am a man under authority, having soldiers under me. And I say to this one, 'Go' and He goes; and to another come, and he comes; and to my servant 'Do this' and he does it.

Just as the officer had authority over his soldiers, he knew that Jesus had the ultimate authority over life. With the authority structure in place Children are commanded to obey their parents and the apostle draws attention to the 5th commandment to remind the church of order and authority.

The 5th commandment is the law of authority. It prescribes the honor that children owe to their father and mother. The word honor is particularly important. The word honor comes from a Hebrew word which is often translated glorify in the Old Testament. The root word literally refers to heaviness or weightiness of character. Given the grammar associated with the word honor in the context with which it is used, it means nothing less than reverence of the highest degree. The father and mother are to be honored in the same way, but not the same degree, in which Christians fear and reverence the Lord our God. Honor seeks submission to authority.

Historians may trace the collapse of our society to the breakdown of order and authority in the home. If order and authority cannot be maintained in the home, order and authority cannot be maintained in society.

Now I will proceed to a portion of God's word that is not likely to be received with any enthusiasm. It has to do with the whole matter of slavery. On more than one occasion I've been asked if slavery was biblical. I cannot find in Scripture any direct or indirect condemnation of slavery. In fact the Bible is very clear about how slaves and masters live together in a Christian society.

The regulations set forth by Moses in Exodus 21:1-11 and Leviticus 25:39-55 as well as numerous other places applied to the economy in theocratic Israel. However, the general equity of those principles is present in the New Testament.

The Greek word translated servant or bond servant is *doulos*. It signified ownership. The New King James Version translates it to the English word slave. Paul used this word to describe himself (Romans 1:1).

The Bible had a name for the hired servant. The Greek word that describes the hired hand is *misthotos*. James the son of Zebedee and John his brother were mending fish nets with the hired servants. Paul did not consider himself a hired servant of Jesus Christ. Today we think of a servant as one who is paid to carry out the mundane chores of life. We hire such a one to cook, clean the house, cut the yard, etc.

There is another word used in the text of the Greek New Testament manuscript that describes a servant and that word is *therapon*. This word describes one who performs a service in the interest of public good. For instance Hebrews 3:5 states "Now Moses was faithful in all His house as a servant, for a testimony of those things which were to be spoken later." Paul was not just a public servant for the good of mankind.

There is another word used in the Greek text that describes a servant. The word is *huperetes*. This word describes one person who is subordinate to another person. That does not fit Paul's description as a servant.

One other word is translated servant in the New Testament from the Greek word *diakonos*. Most often we translate it as deacon but it is also translated servant such as when Paul describes Epaphras in Colossians 1:7. The idea is that Epaphras served in the church as a deacon in a way similar to the way a deacon would serve in the church today.

All these words except *doulos* represent a master/servant relationship. There is nothing humiliating in any of these terms, but the word slave (*doulos*) is humiliating. The English words bondservant or servant in Paul's letter to the Romans takes away from the original Greek word, which is slave (*doulos*). Even though a slave may achieve a high position in life such as the very responsible position held by Nehemiah or Daniel, the high position did not remove the stigma of slavery.

Paul was a Hebrew of Hebrews and a Roman Citizen. He held dual citizenship (actually triple citizenship when we consider his citizenship in heaven). A man who held his honored civil position would never have submitted himself a slave to another human being. However, Paul was happy to be called a slave of Jesus Christ (Romans 1:1 and Philippians 1:1). Paul was happy to be called a slave to the one who not only created him, but who redeemed him from his fallen estate. Truly it may be said that when one is a slave of Jesus Christ, that one has the truest liberty and the highest dignity.

The question remains, who wants to be a slave? No one unless the institution functions according to God's law. But under God's law it is not a bad institution at all, if fact, if perfected it appears that Paul prefers biblical slavery over against secular freedom.

The Bible legislates the manner in which the master and the slave relate to each other. Read Philemon. There you will not find the abolishment of slavery, but quite on the contrary one could read that short letter and conclude that slavery was a norm of society that only needed to be regulated by the Word of God. The Bible does teach the masters to treat their slaves with fairness and justice (Colossians 4:1).

If the institution of slavery has been presented as an immoral institution, the clearest of reasoning has been abandoned and words of Holy Scripture disregarded. The Bible does teach that cruelty, abuse, tyranny, and injustice are immoral to the core. Human governments have been cruel, abusive, tyrannical and many immoral to the core. Government, football, ping pong, home cured sausage and slavery are not sinful just because they exist, but they may become sinful if they become objects of worship or they are not regulated by God's Word.

We are all slaves.

> Do you not know that when you present yourselves to someone as slaves for obedience, you are slaves of the one whom you obey, either of sin resulting in death, or of obedience resulting in righteousness. (Romans 6:16)

Slavery is a fundamental concept that Christians are not free to dismiss. The institution of slavery regulated by the Word of God brings with it a sense of belonging, a sense of community. The kind of freedom sinful man seeks is an independent spirit. I want to be my own self. I want to control my own life.

There is a story told about a slave who despised the thought of being owned by an Englishman. The slave said he would never obey so unworthy a master. However after the purchase the slave learned that his new master had purchased him to give him his freedom. The poor slave was so overwhelmed by joy and gratitude he said, "I am your slave forever."

The Psalmist understood the servant/master relationship.

> O Lord, truly I am Your servant; I am Your servant, the son of Your maidservant; You have loosed my bonds. I will offer to You the sacrifice of thanksgiving, And will call upon the name of the Lord. (Psalm 116:16ff)

Paul's inspired letter is to Christians, and therefore to Christian masters and Christian slaves. The Bible gives the church ultimate design needed to maintain mutual order and respect for those of authority and those who are subordinate to that authority. The parent, the schoolmaster, the teacher, the pastor, the ruling elder, the employer and employee, the government official or even the slave and the master are examples of those who may hold offices of authority. When Christians refuse to submit to the authority God has placed over them, they mock God with contempt and disrespect.

God's authority does not include cruelty, abuse, tyranny, and injustice. If professing Christians are slaves to sin, then cruelty, abuse, tyranny and injustice will follow them. If Christians are slaves to righteousness then they will find the glory of God in order and authority.

22. The Grace of God in His Glorious Power

Ephesians 6:10-20

Reading this text may lead one to believe the church is at war. It's not just this text. The following list should be examined carefully.

> God's people, the visible church, hear the fire breathing threats of the enemy, who has no conscience.
>
> The church is under siege. The egalitarians and special interest groups hate the church.
>
> A totalitarian state is on the rise, which will bring more restrictions and regulations to the church.
>
> Our nation faces cultural and sociological bankruptcy.
>
> All kinds of malicious new age movements despise the church of Jesus Christ.
>
> The liberal news media looks for every opportunity to criticize the church.
>
> Materialism and consumerism continues to dominate the lives of Christians and unbelievers alike.
>
> Doctrinal standards have been and will continue to be lowered because of a desire to be seen as a loving people in a pluralistic, democratic, postmodern culture.

Confessional standards have been dumped in favor of charismatic church leaders with alleged supernatural gifts.

The success syndrome has turned pastors into chief executive officers.

Christians have slowly, but surely, been desensitized to sin. False teaching in seminaries will continue to soothe the wounds of sin rather than doing the hard job of teaching, preaching and holding Christians accountable.

Fear of confrontation will allow sin to go unchallenged.

More and more Christians simply refuse to submit to the Word of God as the only rule of faith and practice.

The desire for acceptance and unity has mutilated the marks of the evangelical church.

An emotional religious experience is the norm to establish morals, ethics, doctrine, and theology.

More and more professing Christians claim "God is not rational."

Considering the visible church in a general sense, are my assertions true or not? If what I've said is true where is the glory of God in the visible church? Like every generation of Christians, we find ourselves looking for the glory of God, but seeing the hand of the enemy.

The Old Testament saints faced the same problem. "Then the glory of the Lord departed from the threshold of the temple and stood over the cherubim" (Ezekiel 10:18). "And the glory of the Lord went up from the midst of the city and stood on the mountain, which is the east side of the city" (Ezekiel 11:23).

When Paul wrote this letter to the Ephesian church, he had the glory of God in mind as the main theme of the letter and the theme of this text. However, the enemy would make every effort to destroy God's glory.

This Portion of God's word begins with another command, "be strong in the Lord." If your understanding of the Bible is man-centered, such as Arminians, charismatics and others tend to be, you might be tempted to think you have the power to stand against the enemy. You don't.

When the English Bible commands Christians, "be strong" it sounds as if it is an action they have to produce. It is not. It is almost impossible to convey the use of the Greek verb into sensible English. Literally it is "be ye being empowered." The power to stand against the enemy is from God. "It is God who works in you both to will and to do for His good pleasure" (Philippians 2:13).

When God empowers the church to stand against the enemy, Christians will then be able to put on the whole armor of God. Christians ought to realize they have an enemy. The enemy is the devil. He is described as a ruler, an authority, an evil one and one who lives in darkness. The thought of a personal, persuasive, and powerful devil has almost been dismissed by the majority in the modern church. I've heard people say, "the old devil, spooks, and witches were the pre-modern ignorance of Roman Catholicism and those weird Puritans."

From the Bible it is abundantly clear the devil is a real person. "Resist the devil and he will flee from you" (James 4:7). The Apostle Peter referred to him as, "Your adversary the devil, prowls about like a roaring lion, seeking someone to devour" (1 Peter 5:8).

Christians must not underestimate the power of the forces of evil that exist in this world. Those who are under the power and influence of Satan, though they live in this physical world, are enemies against whom Christians must do battle. When Christians use language like battle, war, fighting, they are using military metaphors. The inspired apostle uses them as well. Christians are fighting a spiritual battle, but a very real battle, so they have to use language appropriate to the cause.

A warrior must have the ability to stand. You cannot fight a war sitting down.

> Therefore take up the whole armor of God, that you may be able to withstand in the evil day, and having done all, to stand. Stand therefore, having girded your waist with truth, having put on the breastplate of righteousness, and having shod your feet with the preparation of the gospel of peace; above all, taking the shield of faith with which you will be able to quench all the fiery darts of the wicked one. (Ephesians 6:13-16)

Today military men are issued the best equipment available, so when the battle is over the soldier will still be standing. The Roman soldier's armor was his *panoplia*, which consisted of his whole armor. Three essential parts of the armor are mentioned in our text. The belt was foundational to all the other gear. The belt gathered the short tunic and kept the breast plate in place. The breast plate covered the body from the neck to the thighs. His *panoplia* protected the vital body organs, except for the head, so the soldier had a helmet to protect the head. Then boots were needed to make the long marches over rough terrain.

These metaphors describe the protection needed to fight the inevitable spiritual war that Christians must fight. First, you need the foundation to all other equipment and that is the truth. If you enter spiritual battle without the truth, you will end up on the ground, either wounded or dead. Hypocrisy is deadly and if you fight without truth you will end up like Demas, who was a deserter. Second, you must have "the breastplate of righteousness." There must be a devout and holy life accompanying the truth of salvation. Third, you must have a good offense. You must be prepared to attack the enemy with the gospel. The message of reconciliation is possible only by the blood of Jesus Christ, who died to save His church.

Christians find the truth to fight this spiritual battle in the Word of God. They cannot understand how to live a holy life without the Word of God. They cannot know and understand the gospel except from the Word of God.

The glory of God is demonstrated by His glorious power as he gives Christians victory over their enemies.

23. The Glory of God's Benediction

Ephesians 6:21-24

The world is full of chaos and confusion. The church is full of chaos and confusion. Children are killing each other, adults acting like children, a nation pilfering its citizens, churches despise the doctrine of Christ, even evangelical churches prefer evangelical unity over sound teaching of Scripture.

Christians cannot escape this chaos and confusion, because they live in this world and minister in the church. Sooner or later Christians get accustomed to the chaos and confusion and opt to overlook it, try to ignore it, or simply get used to it. The chaos and confusion is still there and there are times when it emerges with great fury, but most of the time individual Christians suppress it and go about their business. Who knows, maybe one day it will go away.

Every fashionable aberration known to man including all presumed psychological, sociological, or philosophical discoveries sets the agenda to sooth the pain and hurt that comes from chaos and confusion, however none of them brings order and harmony to our lives.

One of the reasons Christians want to gather and worship God together is with the hope of escaping this mixed up world, if even but a short time. The church worships God by singing Psalms and hymns, confessing their faith, and praying to the only true and living God. They also want to hear the Word of God and hear God's appointed ordained minister of the word preach the word. It helps them escape from the chaos and confusion.

Every local particular church should ask this question: Is our motive for being here the glory of God or has the glory of

God in worship been abandoned for the sake of evangelism, revivalism, moralism, and a dozen other man-made religious cults. Some are so hardened to the chaos and confusion in this life that worship on the Lord's Day doesn't find its proper place in the heart. It is for that reason the glory of God's benediction is so important to the individual Christian as well as the church collectively.

If I conducted a poll of evangelical Christians with the question: Why is the benediction important to you, I would probably get a variety of answers. The one answer that would surely top the list is "the benediction tells me the worship service is about over." Personally the benediction is the most important part of the worship service. It is the primary part of worship that actually helps me deal with the chaos and confusion that I face day after day.

I need to clarify any possible misunderstanding you might have about the benediction. For a long time I thought the benediction was a benevolent prophecy. For the next week I expected good things to happen (a happy life), because that is the meaning of a blessing, isn't it. If we're thinking in materialistic terms, which most people do today, the blessing of God means plenty of material things and lots of happiness. However, God's benediction has nothing to do with material things or even your happiness for that matter.

Plain and simple the benediction in worship is a blessing pronounced by God's ordained minister for the people of God. What is the nature of this blessing? Many professing Christians think of a blessing as something good coming their way. The watershed effect of such thinking has distorted the blessing of God's people in the benediction. The inspired apostle Paul announced the benediction to God's people at the close of many of his letters to the churches. He employed different words, but the essence of his benedictions are the same.

Ephesians

The benediction Paul used in His inspired letter to the Ephesians is particularly comforting because it is from God the Father and the Lord Jesus Christ. God's benediction includes peace, faith, and love.

God has given his church peace. First the church has peace with God through the Lord Jesus Christ. Then what naturally follows is peace with God's children. Then love with faith because love comes from faith. As our faith increases our love for God increases. Peace, love, and faith are gifts from God. These gifts come to us through the Lord Jesus Christ, the Mediator of all spiritual blessings.

The benediction is the one time in the worship service that the worshipper can understand and experience God in a most intimate way. It is the zenith of all human experience. Yes the benediction is the summit of our religious worship. The benediction gives the church a glimpse of God's glory. That is what God's benediction is all about. God's benediction invokes his blessing. God's blessing uniquely brings the church before Him.

God's instruments of comfort for the heart are the faithful ministers in the Lord. God has appointed them to announce His benediction so you will realize that the chaos and confusion in your life is temporal and will end when God calls His church to Himself.

The reason for the chaos and confusion in our lives is because of the instability and lack of confidence we have in reality. Unfortunately some Christians seek satisfaction in the things of this world rather than the things that belong to God in the spiritual world. For example, the beatific vision of God is rarely mentioned in sermons but it explains the appearance of God; to see God as He really is. God had revealed Himself to Moses in the burning bush and the Red Sea opened and food miraculously furnished, but Moses was not happy.

Moses pleaded with God, "please show me your glory." God replied, "I will put you in the cleft of the rock, and will cover you with My hand while I pass by. Then I will take away My hand, and you shall see My back, but My face shall not be seen." No man can see the face of God and live.

We want to see God, but we can't see God, so we try to fill that void with thousands of idols, thoughts, and ideas. Why do preachers not preach on the beatific vision of God? I don't know. But I do know this, if we spent more time preaching on the beatific vision, we'd see the glory of God in His benediction in a fuller more complete sense.

In the absence of seeing God's face or even the absence of theophanies (the burning bush) God prescribed a benediction to be announced by God's minister to the congregation of God's people. We find the clearest prescription for God's benediction in Numbers 6:22-26. This is typical Hebrew parrellism. The same thought is conveyed in a different way in each individual stanza.

> The Lord bless you
> The Lord make his face shine upon you
> The Lord lift His countenance upon you

The Lord's presence is the Lord's blessing. It is the sacred presence of God that will dispel the chaos and confusion in this world.

> The Lord keep you
> The Lord be gracious to you
> The Lord give you peace

Not only His presence, but His peace that brings order and harmony to your life. God invites his people into His presence in a collective worship service on the Lord's Day. They should take great pleasure in godly worship. The church is not an entertainment theater. Worship does not have man in mind. True worship is God centered.

Ephesians

God brings His church into His presence, gives them His peace, and sends them away with His benediction. The intellectual and emotional capacities should be exercised to the maximum when the church hears the final words in the benediction to the church. "Grace be with all those who love our Lord Jesus Christ in sincerity" (Ephesians 6:21). Grace marks God's benediction to God's people who love the Lord Jesus Christ with imperishable love.

About the Author

Martin Murphy has a B.A. in Bible from Columbia International University and Master of Divinity from Reformed Theological Seminary. Martin spent nearly thirty years in the class room, the pulpit, the lectern, the study, and the library. He now devotes most of his time consolidating academic and practical gains by writing Christian books. He is the author of twenty Christian books on topics such as apologetics, theology, and biblical exposition. He and his wife Mary live in Dothan, Alabama.

More Books by Martin Murphy

The Church: First Thirty Years, 344 pages, ISBN 9780985618179, $15.95
This book is an exposition of the Book of Acts. It will help Christians understand the purpose, mission, and ministry of the church.

The Dominant Culture: Living in the Promised Land, 172 pages, ISBN 970991481118, $11.95
This book examines the culture of Israel during the period of the Judges. It explains how worldviews influence the church and it reveals biblical principles to help Christians learn how to live in the culture.

My Christian Apology, 98 pages, ISBN 9780984570874, $7.95
This book investigates the doctrine of Christian apologetics. It explains rational Christian apologetics.

The Essence of Christian Doctrine, 200 pages, ISBN 9780984570812, $12.95

This book was written so that pastors and layman would have a quick reference to major biblical doctrines. Dr. Steve Brown says it was written, "with clarity and power about the verities of the Christian faith and in a way that makes a difference in how we live."

Return to the Lord, 130 pages, ISBN 9780984570805, $8.95

This book is an exposition Hosea. The prophet speaks a message of repentance and hope. Hosea's prophetic message to Old Testament and New Testament congregation is "you have broken God's covenant; return to the Lord. Dr. Richard Pratt said "We need more correct and practical instruction in the prophetic books, and you have given us just that."

Theological Terms in Layman Language, 130 pages, ISBN 9780985618155, $8.95

This book is written so that simple words like faith or not so simple words like aseity are explained in plain language. Theological Terms in Layman Language is easy to read and designed for people who want a brief definition for theological terms. The terms are in layman friendly language.

Brief Study of the Ten Commandments, 164 pages, 9780991481163, $10.95

This book will help Christians discover or re-discover the meaning of the Ten Commandments.

The Present Truth, 164 pages, ISBN 9780983244172, $8.95

Each chapter examines a topic relative to the Christian life. Topics such as church, sin, anger, marriage, education and more.

Doctrine of Sound Words: Summary of Christian Theology, 424 pages, ISBN 9780991481125, $16.95

This explains the doctrine of Christianity in a systematic format for the layperson. It covers a wide range of theological topics such as, the triune God, creation, providence, sin, justification, repentance, Christian liberty, free will, marriage and divorce, Christian fellowship, et al). There are thirty three topics beginning with "Holy Scriptures" and ending with "The Last Judgment." It is a systematic theology for laymen based on the full counsel of God.

The god of the Church Growth Movement, 95 pages ISBN 9780986405587, $6.95

This work includes a brief explanation of modernity and its effect on church growth. It is a critical analysis of the church growth movement found in every branch of the Protestant church.

Friendship: The Joy of Relationships, 46 pages, ISBN 9780986405518, $6.49

This condensed book was written so the reader will be able to grasp the principles without having to go back and re-read it to digest the content. Friendship is a popular concept. Having a large number of friends was popularized by the social media such as Twitter and Facebook. Friendship involves a relationship of distinction. It is a relationship that respects the dignity of another person. The Bible teaches a different version of what it means to be a friend than the popular culture teaches.

Ultimate Authority for the Soul, 151 pages, ISBN 9780986405501, $9.99

This book examines that question and concludes that every rational being has some recognition of God as the ultimate authority. Although God is the ultimate authority, He confers His authority by means of the Word of God. The author examines Psalm 119 to build a defense for the ultimate authority for the soul.

Constitutional Authority in a Postmodern Culture, ISBN 9780985618124, 56 pages, $5.95

This book shows the validity of constitutional authority and the invasion of postmodern theories in western culture. Postmodern theory has assaulted the western culture on the battleground of absolute truth and reality. Postmodern theory places human experience over abstract objective principles. Christians have a constitution known as the Bible so they will know the truth of reality. The last chapter is devoted to cultural reformation.

Learn to Pray: Biblical Doctrine of Prayer, ISBN 9780986405563, 107 pages, $7.95.

This book examines the Lord's model prayer so Christians may learn to pray according to the Lord's instruction. It also reviews some of the prayers of the apostle Paul to discover his doctrine of prayer. Pastor James Perry wrote the Foreword with insight and experience. "I am impressed with this book on the subject of Learn to Pray. It is stated briefly and succinctly following the model and example of the Lord's Prayer. There is considerable practical instruction on the meaning and implication about purposeful and biblical prayer and it will serve as a useful primer for all who apply the prayer principles. The reader will doubtlessly return to the instruction frequently for the practical help it offers."

www.ingramcontent.com/pod-product-compliance
Lightning Source LLC
Chambersburg PA
CBHW071509040426
42444CB00008B/1570